EMPOWERING THE BEGINNING TEACHER OF MATHEMATICS IN
ELEMENTARY SCHOOL

EMPOWERING THE BEGINNING TEACHER OF MATHEMATICS

A series edited by Michaele F. Chappell

EMPOWERING THE BEGINNING TEACHER OF MATHEMATICS IN
ELEMENTARY SCHOOL

Edited by

Michaele F. Chappell
Middle Tennessee State University
Murfreesboro, Tennessee

Jane F. Schielack
Texas A&M University
College Station, Texas

Sharon Zagorski
Milwaukee Public Schools
Milwaukee, Wisconsin

NCTM

NATIONAL COUNCIL OF
TEACHERS OF MATHEMATICS

Copyright © 2004 by
The National Council of Teachers of Mathematics, Inc.
1906 Association Drive, Reston, VA 20191-1502
(703) 620-9840; (800) 235-7566; www.nctm.org

Library of Congress Cataloging-in-Publication Data

Empowering the beginning teacher of mathematics in elementary school / edited by
Michaele F. Chappell, Jane F. Schielack, Sharon Zagorski.
    p. cm. -- (Empowering the beginning teacher of mathematics)
    Includes bibliographical references.
    ISBN 0-87353-559-6
    1. Mathematics--Study and teaching (Elementary)--United States. I. Chappell,
Michaele F. II. Schielack, Jane F. III. Zagorski, Sharon. IV. Series.
    QA135.6.E47 2004
    372.7'0973--dc22

                            2004009009

Printed in the United States of America

CONTENTS

QUESTIONING AND DISCLOSURE

TOOLS

INDUCTION AND MENTORING OF NEW TEACHERS

Position

The National Council of Teachers of Mathematics believes that school systems and universities must assume the shared responsibility for the sustained professional support of beginning teachers by providing them with a structured induction and mentoring program. This effort must include opportunities for further development of mathematics content, pedagogy, and management strategies. Association with a trained mentor who has a strong background in mathematics, mathematics pedagogy, and classroom practice is crucial to this program.

Background and Rationale

"Before It's Too Late," a report of the National Commission on Science and Mathematics Teaching in the 21st Century, recommended that teachers be initiated into the profession through induction programs. In many school settings, new mathematics teachers who may not have strong mathematics content knowledge are isolated and given little support and content-specific professional development. In these circumstances, their students are not afforded the learning opportunities and quality instruction advocated by the Council.

The retention of new teachers continues to be a problem, contributing to the overall shortage of mathematics teachers. A research review by Yvonne Gold found that 30 to 37 percent of new teachers leave the profession within their first five years ("Beginning Teacher Support: Attrition, Mentoring, and Induction," in *Handbook of Research on Teacher Education*, 2nd ed., edited by John Sikula, Thomas Buttery, and Edith Guyton [New York: Macmillan, 1996], pp. 548–94).

Recommendations

- School systems should develop structured induction programs that include mentoring.
- University teacher-preparation programs should serve as a partner with school districts in induction programs by participating in the training of mentors, continuing communication with their graduates, and serving as a resource.
- Mentor teachers should be provided with significant and consistent training and be given additional remuneration or release time for their services.
- Schools should set aside time specifically for the collaborative efforts of the beginning teacher and the mentor.
- District and school administrators should recognize the added demands on beginning teachers and their mentors and should be sensitive in making teaching assignments.
- Districts and universities should offer professional development that includes a strong focus on content knowledge, pedagogical knowledge, pedagogical content knowledge, and a knowledge of *Principles and Standards for School Mathematics* and its applications to the classroom.

(August 2002)

PREFACE
Yes, you have made a great career choice as a teacher!

—Shirley M. Frye

Teaching is a rewarding profession. As you embark on what may be the most important adventure of your life—that is, the process of teaching students mathematics—take comfort in the words of Shirley Frye, NCTM Past President, spoken at the Beginning Teachers Conference held at the NCTM Eastern Regional Conference in Boston, Massachusetts, in November 2002. Have confidence in the knowledge that you have acquired from your educational experiences thus far. Exercise patience with yourself as you strive to achieve higher levels of competence and reach proficiency.

As you begin your journey as a teacher of mathematics, you are likely to encounter challenges—both inside and outside the classroom—that will seem to overshadow the perceived rewards of teaching. Realize that in your early years of teaching mathematics, you will probably have a "large learning agenda" (Feiman-Nemser 2003, p. 27) that may require you to gain more knowledge about the content you are teaching and how best to present it to your students. This agenda may also require that you learn more about the norms of teaching among your colleagues and in your school community. Although obstacles will surface during your early years of teaching, you should view them as unique learning opportunities that enable you to refine your existing skills and polish your daily practices as you progress along the path of mastery in your new career.

To assist you in this process, the Editorial/Author Panel for the Needs of Mathematics Teachers Beginning Their Careers has compiled this elementary school volume to help you reach your full potential as an effective teacher of mathematics, thereby improving the mathematics learning of the students who will be the recipients of your instruction throughout your career. The Empowering the Beginning Teacher of Mathematics series contains three books geared specifically toward elementary, middle, and high school teachers of mathematics. These books have been written both *for* you and *to* you. Several authors present their discussions objectively, with the beginning teacher in mind, but many share their wisdom and insights as if they were conversing with you over a cup of tea. We hope that this level of familiarity will set the tone for your use of this volume.

Our initial charge and primary goal was to develop a resource to which beginning teachers of mathematics could refer and one that they would use often while attending to the many demands of the classroom and the teaching profession in general. We all know that each academic year brings new faces and new demands to the classroom, at times making even veteran teachers feel like beginners again. Thus, we anticipate that this volume may also serve as a source of inspiration for both beginning teachers and their more experienced colleagues.

The Panel has aimed to produce a unique resource that highlights varied contributions in six broad categories: (1) professional growth, (2) curriculum and instruction, (3) classroom-level assessment, (4) classroom management and organization, (5) equity, and (6) school and community. To us, these categories represent the essential domains to which beginning teachers of mathematics must give immediate attention during the early years to establish a firm foundation in the classroom and to pave the way for a long tenure in mathematics teaching. In each category, individual contributions take on different formats, including featured articles, related thematic ideas, bulleted lists of tips and advice, personal testimonies, quick notes that shed light on specific topics, and quotable thoughts that can be stated best only by teachers. Journal-like pages are included at the end of each section for you to make notes and add your personal ideas, stories, tips, or advice to which you can refer in subsequent years or share with colleagues.

From the onset of the writing project, we were careful to avoid producing a volume that mirrors the numerous resources already available in teacher journals and related books. We certainly encourage you, as a beginning teacher of mathematics, to make full use of these resources as you seek to learn more about the situations you encounter in your first few months in the classroom. Our desire, however, is that you do more than merely "read and shelve" this publication. We hope that you keep it close at hand during your early years as a teacher and that you think of it as an *active* resource—one that becomes an integral part of your teaching regimen—in your search for solutions to issues and problems, not solely mathematical, that are sure to arise in your classroom or school during your beginning years.

Numerous people have made possible the production of the books in the Empowering the Beginning Teacher of Mathematics series. I especially offer my gratitude to the other members of the Editorial/Author Panel for their innovative, diligent, and focused work:

- Jeffrey M. Choppin, University of Rochester, Rochester, New York

- Tina Pateracki, Jasper County Schools, Ridgeland, South Carolina

- Jenny Salls, Washoe County School District, Sparks, Nevada

- Jane F. Schielack, Texas A&M University, College Station, Texas

- Sharon Zagorski, Milwaukee Public Schools, Milwaukee, Wisconsin

Throughout this project, the members of the Panel have contributed countless hours reviewing, editing, and crafting supporting segments to prepare this entire volume for *you*—the beginning teacher of mathematics in the elementary school. I also wish to acknowledge Harry Tunis, our staff liaison at the National Council of Teachers of Mathematics (NCTM), for his unwavering support and guidance, as well as the production staff of NCTM for assistance in the editing and production of this work. Finally, I wish to thank the authors, who have contributed to this effort as a response to their own desire to see you develop into an enthusiastic, effective classroom practitioner.

Our hope in producing this volume is that you "emerge from [your] first few years of teaching [mathematics] feeling empowered, supported, and capable in all roles of the classroom teacher" (Renard 2003, p. 64). You can help yourself in this endeavor by recognizing the multifaceted roles and responsibilities that teachers of mathematics assume during their beginning years. Moreover, as NCTM's position statement about new teachers suggests, you should, if possible, take part in a high-quality induction or mentoring program. Ultimately, you should position yourself to reach out to your future colleagues who will enter the field after you and share the ideas that you learn from this volume, other resources, and your own experience.

Yes, you have made a great career choice as a teacher of mathematics in the middle school. Now we urge you to enjoy your journey!

Michaele F. Chappell
Series Editor

INTRODUCTION
Jane F. Schielack
Sharon Zagorski

During the elementary grades, you as a teacher lay the foundation for your students' future mathematical development. You may have responsibility for teaching all subject areas and spend a large part of each day with your students. Thus you may not consider yourself solely a mathematics teacher, but you realize the importance of teaching mathematics. Because the elementary mathematics curriculum has become increasingly more sophisticated, your imperatives as a teacher include helping students make sense of mathematics and enabling them to acquire the skills and insights needed to solve mathematical problems. This effort requires that you continue to understand more about both the mathematics content featured in the elementary school curriculum and the appropriate pedagogy, as well as about how students think at that level.

In teaching mathematics at the elementary school level, your role is to create opportunities for students to learn new mathematical concepts, develop strategies, and build on them. You then help support your students in their learning by asking questions to extend their thinking. You will need to assess what your students know and what they need to know, so that you can make decisions about your teaching practices. All the while, continuing to value students' thinking and reasoning is vital. You accomplish all this by creating a classroom environment that encourages mathematical learning.

Beginning at prekindergarten and continuing throughout the elementary school years, students develop rapidly in their abilities in, and dispositions toward, mathematics. Most youngsters enter the elementary grades eager to learn about the world around them and to make sense of it through reasoning and problem solving. They are active, resourceful persons who learn by constructing and modifying their ideas while connecting and integrating this new knowledge with their immediate surroundings. Young students learn by talking, experimenting, and sharing ideas with one another. Eventually they learn to express themselves in writing, as well. Young children have a great interest in, and enthusiasm for, learning mathematics. Therefore, you, the elementary school teacher, should work to maintain their enthusiasm and help them grow as mathematical learners. As young students continue to grow mathematically, helping them learn to work together as a community of learners becomes even more important. This book has been designed to help you, the beginning teacher of mathematics in the elementary school, operate effectively in supporting your students in their development of rich mathematical thinking. Section 1, "Professional Growth," highlights the importance of continuing your own learning in both formal and informal settings as you gain more experience as a teacher. Section 2, "Curriculum and Instruction," addresses major components of implementing the curriculum through well-designed instruction: planning tasks to include opportunities for mathematical thinking; enhancing such tasks through well-developed questioning strategies; and incorporating appropriate tools in the lesson to support mathematical thinking. The articles in section 3, "Classroom Assessment," allow you to think about different ways to learn what students know and are thinking about. Section 4, "Classroom Management and Organization," includes ideas related to a major question held by most beginning teachers—"How do I make things work for me and my students?" To assure that you consider all your students in this question, section 5, "Equity," addresses the important issues of diversity and establishing equitable situations in your classroom. Finally section 6, "School and Community," reminds you that the school environment is only a part of a larger community that involves parents and other interested parties; this section presents suggestions for obtaining their support.

More likely than not, your first year of teaching will leave you with many memories—some containing ideas that you will want to revisit and others containing experiences that you wish never to encounter again. However, from each experience you can learn to be a better teacher of elementary school students. As you get under way with your first year in the classroom, we hope this book will provide you with helpful advice toward, and foster your development into, becoming an effective teacher of mathematics.

1 SECTION

Professional Growth

Your first years of teaching will be challenging and rewarding—and stressful. You, as a new entrant to the profession, are expected to assume the same responsibilities as a twenty-year veteran, including everything from operating the copy machine to teaching reform-based curriculum. You may need to adapt and develop lessons, discover how to use new materials, determine the most effective classroom-management skills, and meet the needs of diverse students. As a teacher, you should continuously experiment with new methods and try to learn from your successes and mistakes. We should all strive to do so! As you face the realities of teaching, you may wonder where to turn to continue your professional growth. The following paragraphs suggest several novel resources for beginning the professional development that should take place throughout your career.

Self-Assessment

Reflecting on your own teaching is a vital step in your growth. Analyze your lessons, and think about what went well and what you might change. This reflection can lead to improved lesson planning and teaching practices. Keeping a journal is one way to record your reflections. Some questions to ponder include the following:

- What did I do in my lesson?
- What were the goals for my lesson?
- Did I accomplish my goals?
- What anticipated challenges did my students face during the lesson?
- What were some different ways of thinking that I observed as my students worked on a given task?
- How might I revise this lesson in the future?

Your Colleagues

Collaborating with fellow teachers is another way to grow professionally. Find colleagues who are knowledgeable and willing to share ideas that work. Of course, not all strategies that are effective for an experienced teacher will work for you. Be selective. Seek out new ideas and resources. Ask questions. And remember to share with others what works for you!

Support Groups

Many schools and districts offer formal induction programs and support groups for beginning teachers. Often groups of new teachers meet weekly or monthly to share common concerns and successes. Mentoring programs are also becoming more popular. Consider selecting and working with a mentor. Be willing to seek out more formal support groups. You do not have to face all your challenges alone!

Professional Journals and Organizations

Keep up with current practices and issues in education by reading professional journals. Find time each month to read one or two articles that interest you. Local, state, and national organizations hold annual meetings, academies, and workshops to help you grow professionally. Learn more about what conferences are offered in your area, and attend a conference or workshop to see how valuable such gatherings can be.

Coursework

You may have graduated only recently, but more coursework may be in your future. In the months to come, you might consider expanding your knowledge of mathematics content and pedagogy, as well as classroom practice, through some form of teacher education. Take time to investigate programs, and talk to others in your field about appropriate coursework for the topics in which you are interested.

Although this entire book is intended to provide support and ideas for your growth as a teacher of mathematics, this first section deals specifically with your professional growth. As you read the pages ahead, consider the following questions:

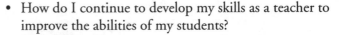

- How do I continue to develop my skills as a teacher to improve the abilities of my students?
- Where do I turn for feedback and advice on my teaching?
- How do I make my first year of teaching successful for me and for my students?

We believe that the habits of reflection you develop as you read this book and think about these questions will serve you well as you seek to achieve growth in your teaching career.

Photograph by Makoto Yoshida.

Four Crucial Insights for First-Year Teachers of Mathematics

Steve Leinwand

In light of the typical absence of collaborative mechanisms to "learn the ropes" of teaching—particularly the teaching of mathematics—I offer this set of four crucial insights for thriving as a beginning teacher. These insights are gleaned from extensive discussions with first- and second-year teachers and from the review of many professional performance portfolios. Moreover, they arise out of a desire to extend the "wisdom of practice" garnered by experienced teachers but shared too infrequently with those who are new to the profession.

Insight 1 Just because it worked once …

One of the most discouraging realities of teaching is that even though a certain approach worked first period, you have no guarantee that it will work fifth period. Conversely, just because something was a disaster this year or during your last-period class, you have no reason not to try it again next year or during a different period. The fact is that classroom dynamics and the distinctive personality of each student and class are often far more powerful determinants of the success or failure of a lesson than your plans. The excitement of teaching—even after years of practice—arises from the unique set of circumstances that you face every year with every new class and from the ongoing struggle to refine and modify your methods. This perspective helps you overcome the daily frustrations and the inevitable classes that "bomb."

Insight 2 Mistakes happen

Another aspect of teaching that is seldom discussed is how rare the "perfect class" is. In fact, you learn quickly that teaching a forty-five-minute class without making at least two mistakes is almost impossible. One mistake is usually a careless mathematical error made because you are thinking several steps ahead. Sometimes your students will catch the mistake, and sometimes the error sits on the chalkboard unnoticed until the classroom erupts in a disagreement about the final answer. The second mistake is usually pedagogical and results from calling on the wrong student at the wrong time or assigning the wrong problem at the wrong time. Either error is sure to engender confusion. When a supervisor or principal is in the room or when you are using technology, the likelihood of mistakes increases significantly. Once you realize that such mistakes are typical in all classes and almost inevitable during any given class, you can begin to shift your perspective and see most mistakes not as embarrassments but as welcome learning opportunities for both you and your students.

Insight 3 Do not try to work alone

The professional isolation of teachers is among the most serious impediments to improving practice and developing teaching skills. Unfortunately, most teachers practice their craft behind closed doors, minimally aware of what their colleagues are doing and usually unobserved and undersupported. Perpetuating this debilitating culture is irrational. Instead, you should realize that remedies for nearly every teaching obstacle reside among your colleagues if you are only willing to ask. As lonely as you may feel in your career, you are not alone. Through direct communication with colleagues, online interaction with other teachers, or the range of professional development opportunities offered locally and regionally, support and helpful suggestions are readily available.

Insight 4 If you do not occasionally feel inadequate, you are probably not doing the job

Just think about what you are being asked to do: teach in distinctly different ways from how you were taught mathematics; use hardware and software that did not exist a few years ago; make much more frequent use of group work; focus as much on problems, communication, and applications as on skills and procedures; teach groups of students that are far more heterogeneous than those of your predecessors; and assess understanding in more authentic ways. Feeling overwhelmed by this torrent of change is neither a weakness nor a lack of professionalism. It is an entirely rational response. A reasonable perspective is that an occasional sense of inadequacy is both inevitable and typical and should be channeled into stimulating the ongoing growth and learning that characterize the true professional.

Keep these insights in mind as you begin your career as a teacher; doing so may save you the sometimes-painful experience of learning them on your own.

I NEVER LEARNED

SEVEN THINGS I NEVER LEARNED IN METHODS CLASS

Margaret R. Meyer

1. Do not think that students never notice what clothes you wear or when you last cut your hair. They are quite observant about such things because these concerns are very important in their own lives. When building a professional wardrobe, do make the choice of comfort over fashion, especially when you are buying shoes.

2. Do not bore your friends with school stories unless they are teachers, too. A story that is funny to a teacher is often not funny to those in other occupations. Do try to balance your life with friends who work outside of education.

3. Do not take your health for granted when working with children. Keep a box of tissues on your desk, and insist that students use them. Ask students to bring in replacement boxes from home; they are usually happy to do so. Wash your hands frequently.

4. Do not think you will always be twenty-something. Pay attention to saving for your retirement. Take advantage of tax-sheltered savings plans.

5. Do not take too long to recover from your undergraduate degree. Start a graduate program as soon as possible. Doing so will pay off well in the long run.

6. Do not isolate yourself behind your closed door. Find colleagues with whom you can talk, plan, share successes and failures, and continue to grow professionally.

7. Do not ever tell your students how old you are, especially when they ask you directly. Instead, add at least thirty years to your age when answering because that age is how old they really think you are. Do think about retiring when your answer starts to sound believable.

Choosing and Working with a Mentor

Sharon Zagorski

New teachers continuously search for support, resources, and ideas during their first years in the profession to make sense of the realities of teaching. One important source of support, the use of mentor teachers, is becoming more prevalent both nationally and internationally. Finding and working with a mentor is a good idea for almost any new teacher. The following lists highlight important questions to consider when you are looking for someone to fulfill this role in your professional life.

What qualities should I look for in a mentor?

- A knowledgeable teacher who is committed to the profession
- A teacher who has a positive attitude toward the school, colleagues, and students and is willing to share his or her own struggles and frustrations, avoiding the naysayer who constantly complains in staff meetings
- A teacher who is accepting of beginning teachers, showing empathy and acceptance without judgment
- A teacher who continuously searches for better answers and more effective solutions to problems rather than believes that he or she already has the only right answer to every question and the best solution to every problem
- A teacher who leads and attends workshops and who reads or writes for professional journals
- An open, caring, and friendly individual who has good communication skills
- Someone who shares your teaching style, philosophy, grade level, or subject area
- A teacher who is following the path you want to follow, someone with whom you can relate and with whom you share mutual respect

- Someone who is aware of his or her own biases and opinions and encourages you to listen to advice but also to form your own opinions

What should I expect from an effective mentor?

- A mentor allows you to talk without interruptions and listens for your sake.

- A mentor maintains confidentiality in your discussions and interactions.

- A mentor helps you explore options, set goals, and attempt to do things your way, using your strengths and personality.

- A mentor builds on your strengths and avoids trying to transform you into a teacher clone using his or her style.

What are my responsibilities as a new teacher working with a mentor?

- Welcome the mentor's interest and concern.

- Realize that both partners can gain from the relationship.

- Realize that mutual respect, trust, and openness are the foundations for achieving success.

- Avoid a passive role; take the initiative in your own development by specifying your needs, soliciting feedback, and using the feedback without viewing it as criticism or an evaluation.

- Have realistic goals and expectations for what can be accomplished. Be open and sincere.

- Communicate any difficulties and concerns as clearly as possible. Be willing to discuss failures, as well as successes. Understand that learning comes from an examination of both.

- Follow through on commitments, and seek help when necessary. Asking for help is a sign not of weakness but of strength.

- Be honest with your mentor about important feelings. Contribute ideas and a variety of options for overcoming difficulties.

What are the benefits of having a mentor?

- Having a mentor gives you an opportunity to learn from an experienced teacher who shares his or her personal knowledge, experiences, and insights.

- A mentor who helps you understand and cope with written and unwritten rules will ensure that you are quickly assimilated into the school culture.

- Working with a mentor gives you the chance to test ideas, strategies, and tactics in a friendly forum before you try them in a classroom.

- Having a mentor gives you access to coaching and counseling.

- A mentor can help you clarify your career goals by making you aware of local, state, and national professional organizations, thus opening the doors to continuing growth and development.

Your work with a mentor will be as rewarding and successful as you make it. This relationship should serve as a strong foundation for support and future professional growth.

Keeping a Professional Journal

Susan Kyle Arn

As you begin teaching, keep a good professional journal. Once a month, update this journal by noting any professional development meetings you have attended, presentations you have made, professional organizations you have joined, and so on. With the journal, keep any certificates of attendance or completion you have earned and a copy of your transcripts, along with a copy of your evaluation and your current teaching certificate. You may also want to include articles from the newspaper or professional journals that you value or notes on topics of interest in your career. After a few years of teaching, you will need to create a new journal, but remember to keep the old one.

You will be surprised how much you will add to your journal each month. It will also come in handy when you need to update your resume or you begin to apply for awards and grants. This journal will become one of the most important professional references that you have.

Team Teaching in Mathematics

Amy Weber-Salgo

Team teaching in mathematics can be a wonderful experience for you and for your students. Below are some ideas you may want to consider if you are assigned to a team-teaching situation.

Two Heads Are Better Than One!

Team teaching offers a number of advantages for the instructors, including the following:

- By sharing your teaching ideas, your lessons become more powerful. You and your co-teacher will learn a great deal from each other.

- Although occasionally both teachers will lead a lesson, most of the time, one teacher leads and the other is available for other tasks. Such tasks might include helping students who need extra attention, academically or behaviorally; leading small groups of students who need enrichment or reteaching; performing individual assessments; or simply dealing with other classroom duties.

Communication: The Most Important Aspect of Team Teaching

Each partner must be willing to share both the good news and the problems that arise in the classroom. Here are some issues to discuss before you begin working together in the classroom:

- When do you like to plan—before or after school? On the weekends?

- Do your plans detail all the activities for the entire month, or do you just sketch out each day as it comes? Do your plans fall somewhere in between these extremes?

- Do you want to divide the lessons and have each teacher plan only his or her part, or do you both want to know details about each other's lessons?

- How do you like your classroom to appear? Are you a stickler for neatness, or is a little bit of clutter acceptable?

- How do you plan to buy materials that are not provided by the school? Do you want to have a fund to which you both contribute?

- Do you want to combine all your teaching materials or try to keep them separate?

- How do you like to communicate with parents? How often?

- What is your method for grading?

- How do you like the classroom to sound? Can you tolerate a certain level of noise?

- How do you feel about routines and schedules? Are you comfortable with changes? How will you handle spontaneity and teachable moments?

- How will you resolve conflicts?

You might try rating the importance of issues that arise on a scale of 1–10. If the level of importance is a 9 for your partner and a 3 for you, then give in! If it is a 10 for both of you, then keep working to resolve your differences. Chances are, if the issue is of high importance to both of you, then it is also important to your students. Remember, building this relationship with your co-teacher can be a positive experience. Many of your colleagues would rather share the experience of team teaching than handle their classes alone!

TOP TEN THINGS I WISH I HAD KNOWN WHEN I STARTED TEACHING

Cynthia Thomas

10

Not every student will be interested every minute. No matter how much experience you have or how great you are at teaching, you will encounter times in the classroom when no student is interested! The solution is to change your tone of voice, move around the room, or switch from lecturing to some other activity. Maybe you can even use a manipulative to increase the students' understanding and, possibly, their level of interest.

Remember— Write It Down!

Barbara A. Burns

A great way to keep track of plans that did not go well, lessons that took too much time, or specific ideas or exercises that drove a lesson home is by writing them directly on your lesson script. Recalling a good teaching suggestion from a previous year may be difficult unless you take the time to jot it down where you are sure to see it when it is needed.

Keeping a Proper Perspective about Your Students

Duane A. Cooper

One of the greatest professional lessons I ever learned was from a student named Ollie Gary*. This student did everything imaginable to be disruptive and to get under my skin, and he succeeded. I love children—and mathematics—but at the time, I hated Ollie Gary. Other children's misbehavior seemed to be youthful mischief or bravado, but to me, Ollie's antics were mean-spirited and intolerable. After one particularly trying day, I was fuming over something Ollie had done. Then I had a revelation: I taught twenty-nine students who adored me and frequently made their feelings evident; I was crazy to let the one remaining child irritate me. For the rest of the year, Ollie Gary never upset me again. Oh, he tried, but I was able to dismiss his annoying behavior. My resolution to tie my emotions to the many appreciative students I teach remains valuable to me; quite often, I have "that one student" in a class who is difficult in some way, yet I cope.

I have no greater joy in my life than teaching mathematics. My wish for beginning mathematics teachers is that you find the same delight and passion that I find in my teaching. I have three pieces of advice for you: Love the mathematics, love the children, and never let one student get you down.

---

* A pseudonym

Notes:

SECTION 2

CURRICULUM AND INSTRUCTION

Teaching involves many decisions, most of which must be made before a lesson begins. These decisions give teachers an opportunity to reflect on the kinds of learning experiences they intend for their students. As a teacher, you may find yourself deciding such issues as what topic should be the focus of a lesson, how to engage students in that topic, what questions to ask students, how to guide discussions to both encourage participation and advance particular mathematical ideas, and what tools or resources to use. These decisions are important because they influence the kinds of learning opportunities and views of mathematics that your students will have. In this section, you will find ideas to guide you as you contemplate these questions.

This section has three major themes: (1) Planning, (2) Questioning and Discourse, and (3) Instructional Tools and Resources. The themes reflect multiple and mostly distinct facets of the complex decision-making you will face as a teacher. As you design and carry out your instructional plans, you will need to consider and reflect on all three areas to teach mathematics for understanding.

Planning

Most likely, planning will occupy a major portion of your time during your beginning years of teaching. To carry out the day-to-day functions of teaching and to be effective in your eyes and in the eyes of your colleagues and administrators, you must understand the scope and nature of the curriculum that you are teaching and the best methods for implementing that curriculum. Planning requires that you consider both the short-term view—what you plan to accomplish in a given lesson—and the long-term view—what should be the lasting learning outcomes of your teaching, such as instilling a mathematical disposition and an ability to solve problems in your students. In this section, you will find guidance to assist you in planning, including how to determine what you are responsible for teaching, what classroom policies are appropriate and effective, and what instructional strategies to use.

Questions and Discourse

As a teacher, you serve as the representative of the larger academic and mathematical communities, and you control the flow of information to your students and the depth to which they think about mathematical ideas. One important component that defines your role is the kinds of questions you ask students during instruction. These questions can serve to assess students' knowledge and to initiate students into mathematical discussions. Because different forms of questions serve distinct purposes, you will need to consider and balance your short-term and long-term goals in determining whether to ask a question that requires a brief factual response or one that requires an extended response in which students must explain their thinking. Reading this section will help you determine the types of questions to ask, both in planning your lesson and in conducting it with your students.

Instructional Tools and Resources

While planning your lessons, you will need to identify what tools and resources, such as technology and manipulatives, to incorporate and how best to use them. For example, you may need a system for distributing and accounting for manipulatives and calculators or advice on how to design lessons that include the use of computer software. Lessons that integrate calculators, computers, and manipulatives may require a good deal of time; however, such lessons tend to offer different avenues through which students can engage in mathematics. As a beginning teacher, you may want to implement tools and resources gradually as you learn how their use can enhance your students' mathematical understanding.

PLANNING

Useful Questions for Planning Instruction

Lee Anne Coester

When beginning to plan a new unit, or even just a new lesson, skim through the list of components and questions below. They are not necessarily presented in order of importance, and not all points can be addressed in every lesson or unit. However, the more these components fit together, the more powerful your lesson or unit becomes. The more powerful your lesson or unit, the more dramatic your students' learning. The more dramatic your students' learning, the better your students' attitudes are likely to be toward mathematics and its place in their future.

Time

◆ How much time can I devote to this lesson or unit?

Equity Issues

◆ How can I address learning styles, multicultural issues, and gender equity?

◆ What opportunities can I provide for those students who already understand this material or "catch on" before the others?

◆ What methods can I use with students who need remedial work? How can I best reteach the material when necessary?

Curriculum

◆ What are my goals? Can I easily combine certain goals with future teaching?

◆ In what order should I teach my objectives? Has my district or state prioritized them?

◆ What is the best way to teach each with the resources that I have?

Teaching

◆ What mathematics should I understand more thoroughly so that I can present the material well?

◆ What activities can the students do to make the mathematics more enjoyable and to help them realize the usefulness of the material?

◆ How can I make this lesson or unit more discovery-based, inquiry-based, constructivist, or student-centered?

◆ What student groupings or other settings would enhance this lesson or unit?

Learning

◆ What can I do to help my students truly understand this material?

◆ What can I do the make this learning enjoyable and to enhance students' attitude toward this mathematics topic?

◆ How can I help students feel good about their achievements?

Technology

◆ What computer programs could I use to enhance this lesson in any way?

◆ When could I appropriately incorporate calculators into this lesson?

◆ What calculator skills could be taught as part of this lesson?

◆ At what level do my students need to be competent with paper and pencil, and what portion of the lesson or unit could be calculator- or technology-based?

Assessment

◆ How can I assess students' existing knowledge of this material?

◆ What methods will I use to assess students' daily learning? Long-term learning?

◆ How will I assess mental mathematics, calculator learning, and problem-solving capability?

◆ What performance-based assessment could I incorporate?

◆ What standardized tests or local assessment tests will my students take over this material? Could I use the same formats as used in those tests?

Number Sense

◆ What overall number sense is being developed in this lesson or unit?

◆ What teaching techniques can I use to help develop this number sense?

◆ How can I help my students "manipulate" these numbers in their heads to determine exact answers and estimates?

◆ When is it appropriate for students to estimate, and when do they need to do the exact mathematics calculations in this lesson or unit?

◆ How can I help my students truly understand the algorithms needed to master this material?

Problem Solving and Reasoning

◆ Could this unit or lesson be based on a problem-solving approach?

◆ What problem-solving strategies could be incorporated?

◆ What questions can I ask to encourage students' reasoning?

Connections

◆ With what previous algorithms or concepts and real-life knowledge do my students need to be familiar to understand and apply this knowledge?

◆ What connections can I make with their past and future learning to make this material easier for my students to remember?

◆ With what literature or other subject areas can I connect this topic to help make the lesson or unit more understandable?

◆ How can this lesson or unit apply to my students' lives? How can I involve the students' parents or families in this lesson or unit?

Communication

◆ What questions can I ask to encourage my students to verbalize and justify their thinking in class discussion?

◆ Where can I use cooperative work to encourage students to share their thoughts with one another?

◆ Where can the students use writing or pictures or diagrams to clarify or communicate their thoughts?

Representations

◆ What manipulatives or models can I include that will help make the mathematics more understandable?

◆ How can I help my students be aware of and use multiple ways to represent this material?

Time

◆ Which components can I combine or connect to better address the ever-present need for more instructional time?

Getting to Know Your Students—Graphically!

Ruth Shane

Making classroom graphs is an activity that indeed *always works*—whether with children in kindergarten or in the elementary grades. It meets the NCTM Standards as a worthwhile mathematical task, offers a variety of learning opportunities, and it is totally adaptable to the context of the particular children in the particular grade level with their particular needs and interests. It offers a range of connections with other subject areas; it immediately gets across the message that mathematics is about numbers and data and physical representations; it lends order to our experiences; and it is a language for describing things that are important for us to know about the real world.

Learning about students through graphing

Graphs foster successful learning opportunities for children who can grasp organizing principles, as well as for those children who are challenged by important, basic data presentation. Graphs that are introduced in the first weeks of school can be a mathematical way of getting to know your students: how many letters in their first name, their favorite school subject, whether they wear glasses, the month of their birthday.

Gleaning data from student questions

A classroom graphing activity offers children the opportunity to analyze data, from the simplest questions that involve visually comparing two quantities (e.g., as a kindergarten activity, exploring the questions "Are there more boys or girls in our class? How do you know?"), to tasks involving percent and proportion (e.g., as a fifth-grade activity, investigating "What part of the class prefers cheese pizza?"). One natural extension is to use the graphing potential of computer spreadsheet programs.

Incorporating graphing into classroom routines

The classroom graphing activity can be introduced to everyone at the same time with a discussion about the contents of the graph. Children can approach the graph in the course of the day and add their input (e.g., color their favorite fruit and place it in a column; place a simple name sticker in the column representing the number of children in their family). At the end of the day during the whole class discussion, the teacher can summarize the results and ask additional relevant mathematical questions.

Adapting graphing to a wide range of topics

In a classroom with children from a variety of immigrant families, the classroom graph can represent countries of origin. In a unit on the media, children can post their preference for a particular newspaper or television station. In a measurement unit, children can check their heights with a standing ruler in the classroom and then record their data. Weather conditions—cloudy, sunny, rain, snow—can be graphed as a daily classroom activity, noting the date and then noticing trends for the month, the season, and the year.

Using graphing to foster family involvement

The classroom graph activity also works very well for parent-teacher meetings. Children can be encouraged to involve their families in making graphs displaying all sorts of data. Teachers and children can bring in examples of graphs from newspapers and magazines to put their classroom activity in the context of popular use.

Introducing mathematics symbols in a user-friendly task

The classroom graphing activity is a good example of "the media being the message." It is a reassuring entry into using mathematics symbols in a user-friendly task, in which the mathematics being learned feels intuitively clear. Just as we use stories about ourselves to get to know one another, a graph embodies interesting information, a certain healthy anticipation of the results, and a summarizing discussion in which everyone can participate.

Benefiting you—the beginning teacher—*and* your students

Graphing offers you, the new teacher, just enough structure combined with enough flexibility to suit your new class of students. It helps you teach many worthwhile concepts and skills in a crowded curriculum while being engaging to students of all ages and ability levels. You can adapt graphing tasks to myriad mathematics topics as well as forge natural connections with other school subjects. You can use graphing to involve students' families and promote parent-teacher communication. And you can implement it on a "shoestring" budget if necessary. So my advice to the beginning teacher is, Get going with graphing!

Mathematics Centers

Marcia Clafford

The purpose of using learning centers in a classroom is to provide the opportunity for independent study for all students. Centers let students work individually on mathematics concepts that need reinforcement. A new teacher who establishes mathematics centers can monitor students' understanding of a particular concept that is emphasized in a center. If called for, more instruction may be needed to ensure students' understanding of a particular mathematics concept or skill.

Mathematics centers are self-correcting, thus allowing students to monitor their practice on necessary concepts without an audience. The teacher can place individual answers for the mathematics-center activities in a folder on her or his desk. When students have completed checking their work, they can note their responses on their own recording sheets. Centers can help build students' confidence and reduce their mathematics anxieties. Group mathematics centers can be instituted using a game format, thus allowing interaction among students. Such cooperative centers prove beneficial in addressing students' learning styles, because students sometimes better understand the explanation of mathematics ideas or concepts when it comes from a peer.

Before establishing a center, a teacher must demonstrate or review with the whole class a particular mathematics concept that is to be emphasized in a mathematics center. When establishing mathematics centers, a beginning teacher is advised to always begin small. Starting a program with one or two centers is advisable until students feel comfortable with the classroom procedures. Prior to students' working in mathematics centers, the teacher should establish guidelines for their use. Suggested guidelines include these:

- Students may use the centers when their class work is finished.

- Students are to use recording sheets to note the name of center at which they worked and the results of their work. (Recording sheets can be used successfully with upper elementary and middle school students.) The teacher determines the content and location of the recording sheets. As an example, a recording sheet might include the following information: student name, class period, name of center, date used, center results, and space for evaluation by student and instructor.

- Students should try a variety of centers during the semester. Many students use only the centers at which they experience success and feel comfortable; the teacher may need to do some urging to encourage students to try different, more challenging mathematics centers.

- Elementary school students may be placed at specific centers according to identifying cards worn around their neck. Such cards allow the teacher to monitor whether students are working in appropriate mathematics centers according to their cards. The creation of center-identification cards is initially extra work for

an elementary-grades teacher but allows for greater control of student movement.

- Assessment of students' progress in the centers can be accomplished by observation by the teacher, guided by the individual needs of the class and teacher expectations.

The following general suggestions have proved useful when establishing a mathematics center:

- The variety of curriculum topics included in centers should address the needs of all students.

- The level of difficulty should be appropriate to the students' learning styles.

- Centers should relate to mathematics concepts either currently being studied or previously studied.

- Centers should be self-correcting, with the students being responsible for keeping their own records.

- On their recording sheets, students write the names of the center or centers they work on during class time, along with the date and the results of their work.

- Every four to six weeks, students should evaluate their performance in centers on a recording sheet (e.g., their need to vary the centers worked on during class time or their need to work in cooperative groups more often); teachers may want to hold conferences with individual students at this time to review their needs and goals in mathematics class.

- The teacher also writes comments on the recording sheets, using positive statements and suggestions (e.g., "Glad to see you are in class more," "Nice to have you in this class," "Great work this semester"). Personal notations are welcomed by the students also. The teacher should remember that the goals of using centers are primarily to reinforce learning and to let all students be as comfortable as possible when applying their mathematics skills.

The use of mathematics earning centers can prove beneficial to the beginning teacher in addressing the diverse learning needs of elementary school students.

Three Birds with One Stone!
Integrating Mathematics, Reading, and Writing

Connie Dierking

A hurdle to cross for all teachers, beginning and veteran alike, is finding the time to teach all that is expected in a day. Finding ways to integrate mathematics into other content areas will not only ease your "teacher-mind" but will give your students the opportunity to see mathematics as a subject that can cross curriculum lines.

Literature is the core of most primary classrooms. We have at our fingertips a multitude of engaging, exciting books that beckon students to step inside and learn more. On my shelf are books I use in my reading and writing workshop that I find useful in mathematics instruction, as well. By teaching a mathematics skill during my read-aloud language arts lesson, I am able to kill two birds with one stone. By determining both a language and a mathematics target skill, I am able to integrate reading, writing, and mathematics during my read-aloud literacy block. My students soon begin to see that reading, writing, and mathematics can be interconnected. Although I continue to provide explicit instruction in all three areas, demonstrating the connections during read-aloud time is powerful. My students are shown that reading, writing, and mathematics can support one another and indeed are tools they need to succeed as learners.

Primary Mathematics Interest Centers:
Journal Writing

Denise Edelson

After my students have completed their daily assigned work, I like to give them entertaining options for completing mathematics activities. Journal writing within mathematics interest centers is one such option. Because I choose journaling activities that reinforce classroom instruction, my students feel confident that they are able to work independently. They record the activities in their mathematics journals, and I check their work to assess whether they are able to apply the skills that they have learned. Here are some of my favorites:

1. Match trade books with a related mathematics manipulative. Put both items in a zip-top bag with simple directions for the use of the manipulative. In their journals, the students draw a picture or write about how they depicted the situation with the manipulative.

2. Put a carry-out menu, an order sheet, and a calculator in a plastic bag. Instruct the students to write down an order of three items and then to calculate the cost of the food. Glue the completed order forms in the students' mathematics journals.

3. Put sheets of coupons from Sunday's newspaper in a plastic bag. Instruct students to cut out coupons that, when combined, are equal to $1 in value. Paste the coupons in the students' mathematics journals.

4. Have students trace around cardboard rectangles, squares, and triangles. Then have them measure the sides in inches and centimeters. Finally, instruct them to record the measurements in their mathematics journals.

By being given choices for independent work that is entertaining, students not only practice what they have learned but also build their confidence in using mathematics.

Beginning the Mathematics Lesson

Dorothy Y. White

How teachers begin mathematics lessons sets the tone for what students are expected to do. One approach to set the tone is to begin mathematics lessons with questions designed to engage students in the problem-solving process. Such questions as "What do you notice?" "What do you think we are going to work on today?" or "How would you solve this problem?" allow students to share their ideas and thoughts in a nonthreatening manner.

I particularly like to begin mathematics lessons with the question "What do you notice?" because every student notices something. For example, a lesson on money might begin with the teacher showing the class a poster with advertised sale items and their prices. When asked what they notice, some children might name the items and their prices, others might notice how the prices were written, and still others might discuss the notion of sales tax, discounts, or shopping with their families.

Asking students to share what they notice at the beginning of the lesson provides the class with information on how their classmates think about mathematics problems and sends a message to students that their opinions are valued. Allowing students to share their thoughts without judgment also increases the number and variety of responses and allows teachers to assess what students know about particular mathematical ideas. By asking nonthreatening questions at the beginning of the lesson, teachers glean information on where they need to focus their instruction and assessment.

Tap into the Magic of Your Students

Claudia Bertolone-Smith

Here are some ideas on how to find magic in your mathematics teaching:

- Know how each lesson fits into the bigger picture of what you are teaching. For example, if you are teaching a unit about multiplication, each lesson should somehow tie into that goal. Remind and show students how each lesson is related to multiplication.

- Be prepared for the students who will understand a topic right away and those who will need extra help. "I'm done" and "I don't get it" are both valid states of mind when learning mathematics. Make sure that you acknowledge and honor each intellectual state in your classroom, and know how you will help students move on meaningfully.

- If you want magic in your lessons, here is where to find it: in your students. Inside each of them is a curious, investigative, patterning, sorting, and classifying mind. Include them. Ask them what they think. Ask them what they see. Ask them to share their ideas, opinions, and reactions.

TOP TEN THINGS I WISH I HAD KNOWN

—*Cynthia Thomas*

9 If a lesson is going badly, stop. Even if you have planned a lesson and have a clear goal in mind, if your approach is not working—for whatever reason—stop! Regroup and start over with a different approach, or abandon your planned lesson entirely and go on to something else. At the end of the day, be honest with yourself as you examine what went wrong and make plans for the next day.

Journal Writing:
Documenting What Students Have Learned

Shannon Hart

Implementing journal writing in mathematics can enable you to teach your students more effectively. Using journals helps you assess what your students may have learned correctly, improperly, or possibly incompletely. If students' journal writings indicate misconceptions about a lesson, then the lesson should be retaught, perhaps with an alternative teaching approach. Through their journal writings, students can become active participants in their own learning process.

Help to Begin Teaching in a Problem-Solving Mode

Keith Kull

For many years direct instruction has been the pedagogical model in use in many United States mathematics classrooms. This model generally involves a teacher standing at the board and copying from a textbook different mathematical exercises; students are often taught algorithms to solve these exercises. Also, in such classroom, the discourse primarily transfers from the teacher to the students.

Given the long-standing recommendations of the NCTM process and content standards, the education community now has a broader vision of what the mathematics curriculum should encompass. A part of this vision is to incorporate problem solving into the curriculum, as well as to use problem solving as a vehicle for teaching mathematical content. For example, given exercises 1–6 in the next column, a teacher who is seeking to teach in a problem-solving mode could instead ask the questions that follow the exercises.

1.   14 + 29
2.   8 + 35
3.   25 + 18
4.   32 + 11
5.   15 + 29
6.   13 + 30

A. Find two counting numbers whose sum is 43.

B. Find two counting numbers whose sum is 43 and whose ones digits differ by 3.

C. Find two counting numbers whose sum is 43 and one of whose addends is even.

D. Find two numbers whose sum is 43 and one of whose addends is prime.

E. Find two numbers whose sum is 44 and one of whose addends is 14 more than the other.

F. Find two numbers whose sum is 43 and whose two addends differ by 17.

Perhaps the same teaching and learning goals can be met by both the exercises and the problem-solving questions. However, the questions provide increased opportunities for students to engage in problem solving at a level that enhances not only their computation skills but also their mathematical language, communication, and reasoning abilities.

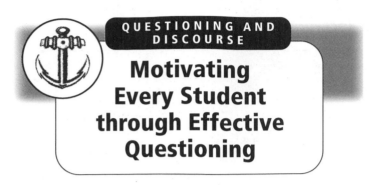

QUESTIONING AND DISCOURSE

Motivating Every Student through Effective Questioning

Jane M. Wilburne

Experienced teachers know that good, motivating questions can help keep students on task, prompt them to think about the material, and give them opportunities to reflect on their understanding of the lesson. Effective questioning engages all students, not just one or two in the class.

To be effective, questioning in the classroom should be used as both an instructional strategy and an assessment strategy. For students, the questions posed by the teacher should enhance their learning and encourage them to become involved in the lesson. For teachers, the questions posed should enable her or his assessment of the students' understanding of the material and the effectiveness of the lesson. If students appear confused and have no sense of how to answer the questions, the teacher should make the appropriate adjustments to be sure that each student understands.

Effective questioning should engage students in an exploration of the material. Questioning should require students to use critical-thinking skills, not simply to give rote answers. Students should be engaged in the learning and challenged by the questioning, and they should assume much of the responsibility for the discussions and explanations that take place in the classroom.

You should prepare high-quality questions at the same time that you plan your lessons. Giving some thought to the questions you will pose helps guide the lesson through an appropriate sequence of activities and keeps you and the students on task.

Keep the summary in table 1 (Wilburne) (p. 20) on your desk to remind you of various questioning techniques of effective teachers, but do not feel that you must master all these techniques in one lesson. Strive to incorporate one technique into your questioning each week. Effective questioning takes time and practice. Keep an index card on which you list various questioning techniques that seemed to work well and those that did not work well. Take time to reflect on how effective your questions were during your lessons. Did they motivate the students? Did they promote curiosity? Did they inspire the students to want to learn more? As you refine your questioning techniques, you will discover that you, too, learn from each question you pose.

Using Learning Logs in the Mathematics Classroom

Roni Jo Draper
Margaret E. McIntosh

Learning logs provide space for students to respond to writing prompts. Our use of learning logs has allowed us to know our students better, to understand their thinking better, to communicate individually with students through the written word, and to reevaluate our instruction on the basis of students' responses. The types and uses of learning logs can vary widely; what follows is a partial list of applications for learning logs in the mathematics classroom.

- Learning logs can be used to open a lesson, readying students for the topic and allowing the teacher to assess students' knowledge of material that is to be presented. Sample prompts might include "What do you already know about slope [or another concept]?" "What do you think you might learn today about slope?" "What do you need to learn about slope?"

- Learning logs can also be used to conclude a lesson, helping students reflect on what they have learned and identify gaps in their understanding after instruction. Sample prompts might include "What did you learn about slope [or another concept] today?" "What questions do you still have about slope after today's lesson?" "How does what you learned today about slope fit with what you already knew about slope?"

- Learning logs compel students to articulate their thinking. The following writing prompts can shed light on how well students understand mathematical concepts: "Choose the hardest problem from today's assignment, and explain how you solved it." "Find the error in the following problem, and explain how to solve this problem without an error." "Solve the following problem in two different ways, and explain why both ways work."

(Continued on page 21)

TABLE 1 (WILBURNE). *Summary of Questioning Techniques*

Ineffective Questioning Techniques	Effective Questioning Techniques
Asking yes/no questions	Asking questions that require short responses in which students must justify their answers, for example, • "How did you know that answer?" • "Can you explain how you found that solution?" • "How can we figure this problem out?"
Calling out a student's name, then asking the question	Posing a question to the whole class, then pausing—for a long period of time if necessary. After the pause, try one of these tactics: • Have students answer the question in their notebooks before you call on someone. • Have students discuss their answers with partners before you call on one or two students. • Inform students that you are going to call on two or three of them, but first, they must all think about the question.
Asking questions that are vague or misleading	Stating questions that are clear and target the learning goals
Answering your own question if no one in the class responds	Requiring students to work in pairs to discuss the question or write down their answers in their notebooks and share their solutions with partners
Asking, "Do you have any questions? Does everybody understand?"	Phrasing questions to determine whether the students understand, for example, • "Who can ask the class a question about the lesson?" • "Each of you should write down one question you have about the lesson. Then, ask your partner." • "Did anyone come up with a question that his or her partner was unable to answer?"
Asking teacher-centered questions, such as, "Can someone explain to me…?"	Asking questions for the class, such as, "Can someone explain to us…?"
Asking questions that require the class as a whole to chant a response; for example, "Everyone, what kind of angle is this?"	Asking questions to help identify which students may not understand; for example, "Identify this type of angle in your notebook. When you are done, look up."
Asking only a few students questions throughout the period	Calling on as many students as possible
Informing a student that his or her answer is wrong	Guiding students through a series of questions to realize their errors
Asking the same type of questions over and over again	Asking a variety of questions in a variety of ways
Talking in a monotone voice	Getting excited and using inflection in your voice; whispering occasionally for effect like you have a big secret
Standing in the same location when asking questions	Moving around the room to make students aware that they are all involved in the lesson
Praising students who answer with a blunt "good"	Using pauses! After a student answers, ask other students what they think, for example, "Do you agree with his answer, Mary? What do you think, John?"

Using Learning Logs in the Mathematics Classroom
(Continued from page 19)

- The following prompts can help teachers evaluate their students' attitudes and biases: "How do you feel about mathematics?" "Why are you taking this class?" "Describe the ideal mathematics class."

- Finally, these prompts can help students reflect on their study strategies and skills: "What do you do when you get stuck on a homework problem?" "How do you take notes for this class, and what do you do with the notes after class?" "How do you prepare for tests and quizzes?"

Students can use about five minutes at the beginning or end of class to respond to prompts, thereby allowing the teacher to read and reply to students' writing quickly. Here are some more hints for using learning logs in the mathematics classroom:

- Use learning logs frequently, at least several times a week.

- Do not accept partial, ill-conceived, or no-effort answers; simply have students rewrite their responses until they have met the standard.

- Respond to students' writing, even briefly, to make sure students know that their learning logs are being read.

Benefiting from Unexpected Discussions

Ji-Eun Lee

Sometimes, students' unexpected responses can generate good discussion topics. This point is illustrated in the following story involving my second graders. In this class, I had an opportunity to hear a productive class discussion that stemmed from a student's unexpected response.

The topics of the lesson were addition and subtraction. I had prepared a lesson plan that contained several practice exercises. However, on this day, the children discussed just the following single exercise:

$$14 - 4 - 4 =$$

Most of the children answered "6," but Alex said that she had an efficient way to solve this problem. Her answer was as follows:

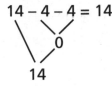

The issue was the order of operations. Alex had computed "4 – 4" first, stating, "Four minus four is easy to compute, so I did it first. Then fourteen minus zero equals to fourteen." Although the other children disagreed with Alex, they could not persuade her that her answer was incorrect. At the beginning, the discussion was a little aggressive. Alex insisted that her method was the easiest way to solve this problem, and the others disagreed with her impolitely. I provided some concrete manipulatives to help with the discussion, but that approach seemed not to work well. Instantly, one child said to Alex, "We cannot take away a part from a part. Fourteen is the whole, and four and four are the parts. If you take away four from four, you take away a part from the other part, not the whole. It does not make sense." Alex then seemed to experience an "aha" moment. She made her own model for this problem and agreed that she should take away the two parts (4 and 4) from the whole (14) to get the answer:

During the next mathematics class, the children continued to explain the addition and subtraction exercises using the part-whole relation that they had discussed the day before. I learned a valuable lesson about an unexpected discussion. Although it may not be included in your lesson plans, it is not a waste of time. It will pay off later.

A Beginning Teacher's Testimonial

One of the first things that I discovered is the importance of posing good questions in class and on tests. Along with open-ended questions, I have had to develop an ability to listen to the way in which my students express their mathematical thinking. Encouraging my students to express their knowledge in terms that are not easily assessed as right or wrong forces me to be a better judge of their thinking processes.

—Travis Olson

Students Sharing Their Mathematical Thinking

Danielle Legnard

My students and I implement a specific process for capturing and sharing how our brains solve mathematical problems. First, I put a problem on the overhead projector for everyone to see. Then each person puts a thumb up when he or she has an answer and a solution strategy to share. While the problem is displayed and students are still thinking, each child's job is to think of the answer and how our brain got to that answer. We wait for everyone while we mentally test our first answer with another strategy to see whether we get the same answer. Students then share how they solved the problem. During the sharing process, students are engaged and constantly checking their own strategies while listening to the strategies of their peers.

This process meets the needs of all my students because it allows them to think in their own way and share what they know. Students who use a variety of strategies are able to challenge themselves; students who have made a mistake feel empowered to fix it; and students who need additional support are able to listen to others who may share an idea that "clicks." This process promotes and supports discourse while students develop sound number sense. As we reflect on the proposed strategies, I hear my students saying to one another, "I wish we could do this all day long!

TOOLS

Maximizing Manipulatives

Thomasenia Lott Adams

The purpose of a manipulative is to help students learn the mathematics. To ascertain whether a manipulative meets this goal I use three steps. First, I explore the manipulative *before* instruction to determine the best ways to use it and to discover any hidden "kinks." Second, I observe students using the manipulative *during* instruction to determine how well these students develop an understanding of a specific topic while using that manipulative. Finally, *after* instruction on the basis of my observations, I assess whether the manipulative met the goal that I set for it prior to instruction. My ultimate goal is to find out whether the manipulative served its purpose to support and enhance students' mathematics learning.

I have developed a grid to help me keep track of the manipulatives that I have available and the concepts for which I have found them useful. When I obtain a new manipulative, I add it to the list. The grid is a flexible tool that can be modified as needed for individual classes or groups of students, and it can be used to choose manipulatives to lend variety, reinforcement, and enhancement in mathematics instruction. Table 1 (Adams) shows my grid for maximizing manipulative use.

TOP TEN THINGS I WISH I HAD KNOWN
—Cynthia Thomas

8 Teaching will get easier. Maybe not tomorrow or even next week, but at some point in the year, your job *will* get easier! Try to remember your first day in the classroom. Were you nervous? Of course; all of us were. See how much better you are as a teacher already? By next year, you will be able to look back on today and be amazed at how much you have learned and how much easier so many aspects of teaching are!

TABLE 1 (ADAMS). *Maximizing Manipulatives*

Manipulatives	Number Sense	Whole Numbers	Fractions	Decimals	Operations	Algebra	Geometry	Measurement	Data Analysis	Probability
Attribute blocks *†	•		•							•
Base-ten blocks *†	•		•	•	•					
Plain/color cubes	•	•	•		•	•	•	•		•
Color tiles *	•	•	•		•		•	•		•
Counting chips *†	•	•			•			•		•
Cuisenaire rods *†			•		•	•		•		
Dot/number dice	•	•	•		•					•
Dominoes *	•	•	•		•					
Fraction circles *†			•				•			
Fraction rods *†			•					•		
Fraction squares *			•				•			
Geoboards *†			•				•	•		
Geometry solids †							•			
Graph paper *†	•	•	•	•	•	•	•	•	•	
Links *†	•	•	•		•	•		•	•	•
Mirrors †							•			
Pattern Blocks *†	•		•				•			
Patty Paper †							•			
Playing cards *										•
Spinners *†					•					•
String †								•		
Tangrams *†			•				•			
2-Color counters †	•	•	•		•	•				•
Unifix cubes †	•	•	•		•			•	•	•
Weights			•					•		

* Transparent form is available for whole-class demonstration.

† Classroom set is available for small-group or individual exploration.

TOP TEN THINGS I WISH I HAD KNOWN
—*Cynthia Thomas*

7 You do not have to volunteer for everything. Do not feel that you always have to say yes each time you are asked to participate. Know your limits. Practice saying, "Thank you for thinking of me, but I do not have the time to do a good job with another task right now." Of course, you must accept your responsibility as a professional and do your fair share, but remember to be realistic about your limits.

Using Manipulatives Successfully

Teaching mathematics with manipulatives can be an exciting adventure. Students learn basic concepts more effectively when they are actively involved in their learning. As they learn each new concept, students, no matter what age, generally go through three levels of understanding: concrete, transitional, and abstract Using manipulatives helps students move from understanding in a concrete sense to understanding abstractions.

When students use manipulatives, they bring their senses into the learning process. Students can touch and move objects to make visual and physical representations of mathematical concepts. They can use manipulatives to represent both numbers and the actions related to the operations on those numbers. Students with different learning styles can use manipulatives to approach a problem in different ways and can spend with the manipulatives the extra quality time that they may require for learning. In addition to meeting the varying needs of students, manipulatives afford the teacher new ways of visiting a topic and different models for explaining a topic.

Although the use of manipulatives can enrich and deepen students' understanding, the use of manipulatives as the sole means of instruction can be ineffective. Students also need formal discussion to form abstractions and make mathematical connections.

If you are looking for guidance on using manipulatives effectively in your classroom, some guidelines are presented in the following article reprinted from the October 1990 issue of *Arithmetic Teacher*.

—Editorial Panel

Jeane M. Joyner

A curriculum with goals for students of valuing mathematics, being confident in their abilities, making mathematical connections, becoming mathematical problem solvers, and learning to reason and communicate mathematically is a call for classrooms in which students are actively involved in learning. It is a call for teachers to establish environments that encourage the use of manipulatives to assist students in attaining these goals proposed by the NCTM's *Curriculum and Evaluation Standards for School Mathematics* (*Standards*) (1989). A major difficulty, however, is how to manage the materials efficiently.

The recognition of the need for activity-oriented lessons to assist students in learning mathematical skills and concepts is not new. Most educators subscribe to the notion that students are better able to internalize concepts and visualize ideas when they work with a variety of models. Why then do so many classrooms remain havens of pencil-and-paper drill to the exclusion of experiential learning?

For the teacher who has never personally learned mathematics in an active manner, the teacher who relies on pages of written work to teach concepts, and the teacher who tried once to use manipulatives only to have chaos, what is needed is not another creative idea but specific guidance in the management of materials. Strategies that are simple and obvious to teachers who successfully use manipulative materials are major hurdles for many instructors.

The following guidelines are generic; they apply to all materials and to all grade levels. And although they seem obvious, they are the missing strategies for many teachers.

Free exploration is a necessity whenever new materials are introduced. Because students' desire to investigate in their own manner is stronger than their desire to follow the teacher's directions, lack of exploration time will jeopardize the best-planned mathematics activity.

To facilitate distribution of the manipulatives, *package the materials* according to the purpose of the lesson. Students do not wait well. If individuals must count out cubes while others are waiting their turns, those at the end of the line will find other ways—usually unacceptable to the teacher—to entertain themselves. Geoboards are easy to distribute, for example, if they are prestrung with rubber bands. Patterning blocks sorted for fraction lessons or boxes with all equipment for an experiment make the distribution of materials go smoothly. Having students help organize the materials can be a learning opportunity. Wise teachers store materials so that students can distribute and put them away with little direction.

When students are involved with hands-on lessons, it is important that *clear expectations* be established for both lesson goals and how students may use the materials. Teachers must be able to articulate their purposes in using the manipulatives. If they do not have a clear understanding of why the materials are important to the lesson, they are unable to help students make the connections from models to an internalized idea. Students build understanding through their experiences. They must be encouraged to summarize their activities and talk about the ideas they discover through the use of the materials.

Students also need simple but clear *guidelines* for what is acceptable and what is not acceptable when using manipulatives. "The cereal is for the graphing activity; you may eat it at the end of the lesson." "When you return your cubes to the shelf, please snap them into sticks of ten."

Finally, teachers should *model the use of materials* and "think aloud" about what they represent. When they see their instructors using manipulatives, students are more likely to value manipulatives and to use them in their own explorations.

Active lessons in which students explore and discuss mathematical ideas are not easy to plan and carry out; assigning a page or two in the book is an easier way to fill the time designated for mathematics in the daily schedule. Teachers who are not currently using activity-oriented lessons need specific ideas on using manipulatives. They need reassurance that the time invested in hands-on lessons is not wasted and will lead to an understanding of relationships between ideas and symbols. Most important, however, staff-development leaders must recognize that teachers who are not comfortable with activity-centered lessons

need *management guidelines* and assistance in organizing their classrooms so that mathematics involving the use of manipulative materials can be implemented effectively.

Bibliography
Focus Issue on Manipulatives. *Arithmetic Teacher*, February 1986.
National Council of Teachers of Mathematics, Commission on Standards for School Mathematics. *Curriculum and Evaluation Standards for School Mathematics*. Reston, Va.: The Council, 1989.

Students Choosing Manipulatives in the Elementary Classroom

I make sure that manipulatives and calculators are visible in the classroom and are easy for students to access. I allow my students to explore these materials when they have free time. Then, when the opportunity arises to use the items to learn about mathematics, the novelty has worn off, students are familiar with them, and the materials serve the purpose intended. When solving problems, I allow my students to select the tools that they think will help them. By watching what materials my students select and how they use them, I get glimpses into their mathematical thinking, including their problem-solving abilities. Sometimes I even learn new ways to consider a problem!

—*Gail Englert*

Mathematics Learning with Technology

Ed Dickey
Melina Deligiannidou
Ashley Lanning

The purpose of using technology is not to make the learning of mathematics easier, but richer and better.

—*Alfinio Flores*

The first axiom in technology planning is, Let the mathematics drive the lesson. Look for ideas that allow you to use technology to enhance your students' understanding of the mathematics they are learning. Avoid teaching technology for the sake of technology. Try to attend an NCTM or a state mathematics conference; both abound with sessions in which experienced teachers explain and demonstrate how they use technology with their students.

Remember to start small but to *start*. If you incorporate technology just once a semester in each class you teach, you are making progress. By adding one more technology lesson each semester, you can, within five to ten years, become an exemplary technology-using teacher.

Students often need orientation to the activity you have planned. Realize that once they are working with the computer, they will no longer be paying attention to you. Technology removes the locus of control from the teacher to the computer, calculator, or group of students using the technology. Plan your lesson in phases. You might begin with an introduction to the whole class. Explain the specific task for students to accomplish or the problem you wish to have them solve. For some activities, you may be wise to pose the problem in vague terms to allow your students a wide range of options, but keep in mind that some students need more structure or direction. A well-constructed worksheet with specific questions can scaffold an otherwise unproductive investigation.

Your role with technology is that of a coach. Resist having students work individually. Working in groups minimizes the number of questions you have to answer and allows students to help one another. Provide opportunities for students to share their work with the whole class. This activity allows you to view their presentations from the sidelines and think about the mathematics instead of what you plan to say next.

Using technology as part of student assessment is a matter of consistency; after all, if you believe that technology enhances learning, then it will also augment assessment. Further, using technology increases the authenticity of assessment, making it more relevant to the world of the student. Performance tasks offer an effective method for using technology in assessment.

Regardless of what software you use, students need time and assistance to learn the application. Often, the more powerful the software, the more effort required to learn to use it. Spreadsheet, interactive geometry, and computer algebra system (CAS) software require students to apply themselves to work effectively. Calculators require orientation. Invest class time to ensure that your students develop useful technology skills. This investment will pay off with enhanced learning of both the technology and the mathematics.

TOP TEN THINGS I WISH I HAD KNOWN
—*Cynthia Thomas*

Not every student or parent will love you. And you will not love every one of them, either! Those feelings are perfectly acceptable. We teachers are not hired to love students and their parents; our job is to teach students and, at times, their parents as well. Students do not need a friend who is your age; they need a facilitator, a guide, a role model for learning.

6

Ideas for a Successful Mathematics Classroom

Lee Anne Coester

I loved teaching mathematics! The following are ideas that were developed over twenty-eight years of teaching and that I wish someone had shared with me when I first began teaching.

- Join professional organizations, and attend conferences. Read your national and state mathematics standards, and use helpful Web site resources.

- Gather your teaching-idea resources. Surf the Internet. Look through NCTM journals, old classroom workbooks, and previously collected materials. Tear out or make copies of anything you might use. Label an expandable file for each of your outcomes, and fill it with file folders labeled with tasks for that outcome, plus one for tests and one for extra material.

- Check with other teachers in your building and at a nearby college or university about available teacher resources.

- Survey materials you have on hand. Look through mathematics catalogs. Make a wish list, and share it with the administration. Do not let your classroom be without pattern blocks, base-ten materials, and geoboards.

Notes:

3 SECTION

CLASSROOM ASSESSMENT

As a beginning teacher, you have many concerns that you need to address every day. One of your most important concerns is how to determine what your students are learning as a result of their experiences in your classroom. Classroom assessment encompasses much more than simply a test at the end of a unit; it includes every action you take to determine what your students know and understand during every lesson you teach. *Principles and Standards for School Mathematics* (NCTM 2000) states that assessment "should support the learning of important mathematics and furnish useful information to both teachers and students" (p. 11). Assessment should be a component of all mathematics lessons to inform you about your students' learning and guide your instructional decisions.

Uses of Classroom Assessment

Classroom assessment can be a useful tool for both you and your students. Your students can use the information from assessments to set goals and to gauge their progress toward those goals. You can use the information to help make decisions about your teaching. Gathering evidence of students' learning helps you identify those who need additional support or challenges and determine your next instructional steps.

Types of Assessment

Assessments come in a variety of forms, including learning logs, journals, observations, interviews, student self-assessments, performance tasks, projects, portfolios, and more traditional tests. Each assessment technique gives you a different way of looking at your students' understanding; thus, choosing multiple forms of assessment is important in developing a broad picture of what your students know and can do. For example, students can make a presentation to the class about a problem they solved, assess their own use of problem-solving strategies while working on the problem, and select a solution for inclusion in their portfolios.

Planning for Assessment

An essential first step in planning assessments is to identify the mathematics you want students to learn and the evidence you need to gather to determine the extent of their learning. As you plan your lesson, think about what you want your students to learn and how you will know that they have learned it. Assessment should be woven into your lesson as a part of the learning experience. To guide your planning, ask students to write a "K-W-L essay," describing what they *know*, what they *want* to know, and what they *learned*, as you begin and end a unit. Deciding what to assess, what assessment to use, and what you will do with the information gathered from assessment should all be parts of your lesson planning.

Grading Assessments

Grading provides the data you need to use assessments effectively. Different forms of assessment lend themselves to different methods of grading. Sometimes, simply reading and responding to your students' learning logs is sufficient. At other times, you and your students will need to gather more extensive data about their learning. Many assessments can be graded using rubrics. If you choose to use a rubric, consider having your students help you develop the grading criteria before the assessment is given, to clarify your expectations. Be selective in your assessments and how you grade them, however, to ensure that you and your students are not overwhelmed with papers!

As you become more proficient in incorporating assessment into your lessons, gathering and interpreting data from assessment, and using that information to guide your teaching practice, your students will learn more and planning a lesson will become easier and more efficient.

Obviously, classroom assessment is difficult to separate from planning. As a result, you will find assessment ideas throughout this book, not just in this section. In particular, look for ideas in the "Curriculum and Instruction" and "Classroom Management and Organization" sections. As you read this section and think about how you will evaluate your students' understanding, you might keep the following questions in mind:

- What is the important mathematics I want my students to learn, and how will I know that they have learned it?

- What types of assessment do I want to use to gather evidence of student learning, and when is each most appropriate?

- How can my students and I use the data I collect from assessment to improve their learning?

Ways to Get Students' Thinking on Paper:
Recording More Than Just the Answer

DeAnn Huinker and Janis Freckmann

Students' written work provides a window into children's thinking—what they understand and how they approach solving problems. Students should not only record answers; they should also show the reasoning and strategies that lead to those answers.

Example: Lucas's Thinking about Muffins

When asked, "How many muffins do we have altogether in the four packages (each package contained six muffins)?" Lucas, a beginning third-grader, wrote "24" on his paper after some deliberation. The teacher wondered how he had arrived at his solution.

Lucas explained his reasoning, stating, "I know that two sixes is twelve, so I added twelve plus twelve in my head and I got twenty-four." Students in the class also solved the problem by using cubes, drawing pictures, or with other strategies. Shasta skip counted by sixes to eighteen and then counted on by ones to get to twenty-four. Anita made four groups with six cubes in each and then counted them all by ones.

Fostering Students' Writing Abilities

In your class, you will find that students' abilities to solve problems and place their ideas on paper vary greatly. We need to teach students how to record their thinking on paper and cannot expect them to immediately be able to perform this task well. A comment often heard from teachers is that their students can verbally explain their reasoning and tell why and how, but that the richness and depth of students' verbal explanations are not found in their written work. For example, students might write "I counted" or "I did it in my brain" when we really want them to explain how they counted or to detail the various steps in their reasoning.

Helping Students Clarify Their Reasoning

Students need support in learning how to think through the steps in their reasoning, then require assistance in organizing those ideas on paper with words, numbers, or diagrams so that their thinking is clearly communicated. Teachers can begin the year modeling the recording process in whole-class discussions of students' reasoning. When Lucas explained how he solved the problem, the teacher elicited ideas from Lucas and the other students on ways to record his reasoning. One student suggested that the teacher record "$2 \times 6 = 12$" and "$12 + 12 = 24$." Then another student wondered how this answer worked and asked, "Where are the four sixes?" This query lead Lucas to further explain his reasoning, "One twelve is two sixes, and the other twelve is the other two sixes." This clarification allowed the class to further examine his reasoning and to consider how to show it in the written record. Then they discussed ways to record Shasta's and Anita's thinking on paper.

Scaffolding Students' Thinking

As you record a student's reasoning, probe him or her to articulate each step clearly. "What did you do first? How could I show that? Then what did you do? I don't understand how you did that; can you tell me more?" The questioning scaffolds the student's thinking as the teacher models how to organize it into a written record. Give the student an opportunity to evaluate the recording. "Does this recording seem to show how you thought about it? Should we include anything else?" Encourage other students to also examine the recording by asking, "Who understands this strategy well enough to explain it to us in your own words? Does anyone else have any questions about this strategy? Are any of the steps not clear?" The basis for the modeling must come from the students so that it reflects their thinking, not yours. Recording several strategies on the board builds up a helpful repertoire of models for students to use as they write about their thinking.

Using Prewriting Discussion

Another important point is that students benefit greatly from discussing their ideas before writing about them. As students explain their thinking orally, they must clarify and organize the mental reasoning that is occurring in their own minds. Through this struggle to communicate ideas clearly, they establish a better understanding of their own thinking. This process prepares them to record their reasoning on paper. The discussion of students' ideas can occur with the whole class, in small groups, or in pairs. "Turn to your neighbor, and take turns explaining how you solved the problem." When students listen to one another articulate their reasoning and hear different ways of thinking, they are helped to refine the ways in which they explain their own ideas.

Supporting Students' Reasoning and Writing Processes

Students need your guidance in learning how to coherently and fully express their reasoning on paper. Further suggestions to support students in this process are listed in the Theme Box. Writing benefits students because they must organize, clarify, and reflect on their thinking in their attempts to record their ideas on paper. Written records benefit teachers because they provide a window to students' reasoning and can be used as an assessment resource to guide teaching and learning.

Supporting Students in Recording Their Thinking

DeAnn Huinker
Janis Freckmann

1. **Talk, then write.** Have students take turns explaining their reasoning in pairs or small groups, then have them write out their strategies.
2. **Pair thinking.** Have pairs work together to represent a joint strategy on paper.
3. **Step-by-step.** Have students number each step of their reasoning.
4. **Revision.** Have students review and revise their written work just as they do in the writing process in language arts class.
5. **Read it aloud.** Have students read their work aloud to you or to a classmate. Often they will identify by themselves ideas that are unclear and parts that are incomplete.

6. **Audience.** Give the students an audience for their writing, such as, "Explain to a first grader (space alien, cartoon character, parent, principal, teacher) how to solve this problem."
7. **Reference charts.** Record students' strategies on chart paper during class discussions. Post the charts on the wall for students to observe the organization of the strategies and get ideas for new strategies to try.

Problem Posing: What's in a Word

Fiona Thangata

Give students opportunities to write mathematics problems. Solving a problem may involve only applying a recently learned technique, but writing a similar problem requires a deeper understanding of the underlying mathematical structure of the problem. The contexts that students choose for embedding their problems also reflect their interests, concerns, and background knowledge and can motivate students to connect mathematics with their daily lives.

Let *All* Students Show What They Know

To allow *all* students to show what they know, in your mathematics instruction, vary their assessments to include oral and written responses and long-term projects. Clearly communicate your expectations for each assignment in advance.

—*Patricia A. McCue and Jennifer Lana-Etzel*

Notes:

CLASSROOM MANAGEMENT AND ORGANIZATION

Experienced teachers tend to use a variety of methods to manage and organize their classrooms. In contrast, beginning teachers may wander the halls during the days before the start of school, peering into the classrooms of experienced teachers in search of ideas about how to arrange the room for that first day, how to set expectations that keep students on task, and how to keep track of students' work when they do stay on task! As a new teacher, the resources you find to address these concerns will influence your own strategies for management and organization and help you create a pleasant and productive learning environment. During your beginning years of teaching, among your first priorities should be the need to organize your classroom and manage the instructional environment in ways that support, rather than impede, students' learning of mathematics. The following paragraphs highlight some important aspects of classroom management and organization.

Set Clear Expectations

Of course, your students are required to abide by your institution's rules and regulations, but you should also establish expectations regarding how your students should treat one another in the classroom and how they should accomplish their work. Do not hesitate to inform your students of these expectations and the consequences of not living up to them. Be fair and consistent in holding students to these expectations.

Know One Another

Whether you are with your students for the entire school day or for only a single class period, arrange opportunities to converse with them. In the same manner that you are different from every other teacher, each student is also unique. One of the joys of teaching is getting to know each student as an individual. You should also provide opportunities for students to interact with one another. Building a sense of community is one important way to create an effective instructional environment in which students can learn mathematics.

Organize People, Space, and Materials

Try a variety of arrangements for individual and group work to meet students' differing needs and keep them engaged in learning. As you get to know your students, you will be able to select appropriate arrangements for different tasks. Keep in mind, however, that students also need chances to try new methods. For instance, a student who seems to work best alone might be asked to work with a partner on a more complex task to help the "loner" become more comfortable working in a group.

You may also try different strategies to organize your space and materials. Experienced teachers have many wonderful ideas for arranging classrooms, making efficient use of closets, or setting up filing systems. Be on the lookout for new ideas, but always consider them in light of your style and your students' needs. Remember that the goal is for students to learn mathematics; your methods for organizing people, space, and materials should always contribute to—not detract from—your students' learning opportunities.

Manage Time

You will soon learn that in teaching, you never have enough time! As you gain experience, you will develop ways to save more time for instruction. Learn to build natural "breaking points" into lessons that are difficult to teach as a whole in the time allowed. As you become more familiar with the required record keeping, look for ways to reduce time spent on that task, perhaps involving students or parent volunteers. Every few weeks, evaluate one hour of your instructional time to see whether you could make better use of the time by changing some small aspect of classroom management or organization.

Assess Strategies for Organization

Not all management tools will work for all teachers. As you read this section and experiment with different strategies for classroom management and organization, you might evaluate each strategy by asking the following questions:

- How does this management or organizational idea contribute to a classroom environment that supports students' learning of mathematics?

- How does this idea help me better organize my students, space, or materials so that I can use instructional time more efficiently?

- How can I involve students in developing ideas for classroom management and organization to build their sense of ownership in the instructional environment?

Nobody Can Really Take Your Place, but a Substitute Has to Try:
Hints to Make Having a Substitute a Positive Experience

Nancy Powell
Cathy Denbesten

Not knowing when you might need a substitute can be stressful; however, being organized can lessen the stress and enable you to avoid last-minute preparations. One helpful organizational technique is to create a substitute notebook that can remain in your classroom. Label the notebook clearly, and leave it in a prominent place or make sure that a colleague knows where to find it in the event you are absent. Organize and mark sections to ensure that a substitute can understand and refer to the notebook easily.

Information for a Substitute Binder

Suggestions for information to include in the substitute binder are listed below.

- A welcome note that thanks the substitute for coming and provides helpful information, such as the handiest place to hang a coat or safely stash a purse, the names and room numbers of teachers in nearby classrooms who are able to answer general or mathematics-related questions, and instructions on where to find needed lesson-plan books

- Classroom rules and regulations, including suggested discipline procedures and locations of detention or discipline forms and hall passes; clear plastic sheet protectors to house copies of these forms in the binder

- A procedure for getting help or contacting the office

- General procedures for fire drills, tornado drills, injuries, and so on

- Forms that need to be filled out every day, and instructions on where to find them

- A chronological list of class periods, including lunch, and times or days that are scheduled for extra duties

- Accurate seating charts with the name that each student commonly uses and attendance sheets that can be carried out of the classroom in an evacuation. Many grade-book software programs include options for printing seating charts with students' pictures, which can be helpful for substitutes.

- Notes for each class that include—
  - ✓ the names of helpful, trustworthy students;
  - ✓ the names of students who have special medical needs or may need emergency care;
  - ✓ the names of non-English-speaking students or students who are enrolled in English as a second language; and
  - ✓ any other important information of which a substitute should be aware

- Clear, understandable lesson plans with instructions about where to find necessary handouts, materials, and supplies for the lesson; notes or keys for worksheets, tests, or quizzes; and an optional activity for each class in the event that students finish their assigned work

- Special activities that can be used any time of the year in an emergency

- A place to leave notes regarding behavior, absences, accomplishments, and questions, by class

Reminders for Students

Spend a few minutes talking to your classes about your expectations for them when you are absent. Remind students that the reason they are in class is to learn and that they need to use every opportunity to do so whether or not you are physically present. When you return, address any issues documented by the substitute. Do not ignore even minor misbehavior unless you want to hear about more problems the next time you are absent.

Making Group Work Effective in the Mathematics Classroom

Abbe H. Herzig
David T. S. Kung

Group work—sometimes called *cooperative* or *collaborative learning*—has numerous benefits for your students, including—

- enhancing their understanding,

- developing their problem-solving skills through work on complex tasks,

- increasing their appreciation of diversity among their peers, and

- improving their communication and social skills.

By struggling with challenging concepts with their peers, conducting brainstorming sessions, explaining their understandings and misunderstandings, and communicating about their problem-solving strategies, students deepen their understanding of difficult mathematical concepts. Group work also affords you the opportunity to see what your students do and do not understand and to learn about their mathematical thinking and problem-solving strategies—information you can use to help plan your instruction.

Selecting Group-Work Tasks

Group work involves more than just putting students' desks side by side and assigning them to work together. The tasks you give your students should be complex enough to require them to cooperate while providing roles for the group members to ensure that each student remains engaged in the work of the group. That is, you want to promote the students' interdependence for the work of the group and each student's individual accountability for his or her learning. Instead of giving students worksheets of problems to solve, give them complex problems that require them to engage in brainstorming and problem solving together. Avoid tasks that allow students to divide up the project into parts and work individually.

Group Composition

Research shows that when a girl is outnumbered by boys in a group, the boys may exclude her, or she may be relegated to lower-level tasks. She may feel intimidated and withdraw from the work. If you encounter this situation, address it with the students and help them learn to interact more equitably. You can also rearrange the groups to include at least two girls, or no girls, in each group. Boys who are in the minority in a group are less likely to have this problem. Similar problems can arise with students of different ethnic or racial backgrounds. Although research has found that working in diverse groups helps foster students' understanding of others' cultures and backgrounds, teachers should teach students to work together productively and should monitor the work of groups closely to ensure that each student feels comfortable participating.

Some teachers prefer to assign students to mixed-ability groups, whereas others separate students of different

TOP TEN THINGS I WISH I HAD KNOWN
—Cynthia Thomas

You cannot be creative in every lesson. In your career, you will be creative, but for those subjects that do not inspire you, you can turn to other resources for help. Textbooks, teaching guides, and professional organizations, such as NCTM, are designed to support you in generating well-developed lessons for use in the classroom. When you do feel creative and come up with an effective and enjoyable lesson, be sure to share your ideas with other teachers, both veterans and newcomers to the profession.

5

ability levels. Here, the research is fairly clear: both the stronger and the weaker students benefit when they work together; some research even shows that the stronger students benefit more because they enhance their own understanding as they explain concepts to others. Struggling students also learn from observing the effective problem-solving behaviors modeled by stronger students.

Teachers and parents sometimes become concerned that the weaker students in a group will rely on the work of the stronger ones, but remember that the laziest students are not necessarily the weakest ones. "Freeloading" can be avoided with the appropriate selection of tasks that require the input of all students; remember to design tasks that engage all students and hold them all accountable for the group's results. You might try rearranging the groups to place students who are not doing their share in a group together. With no one else to depend on, they may have to get to work.

The Teacher's Role

No single teaching technique is effective in all circumstances, but group work should play a prominent role in mathematics instruction. To determine what works best for your students, you may want to use a variety of strategies, adapting these guidelines to the individuals in your classroom. Keep in mind, too, that your job is not finished after you have planned and launched a small-group session; be sure to interact regularly with the groups and observe them as they work. By circulating through the classroom and sitting with each group for a while, you can see which strategies are useful and which are not and adjust the groups or the tasks accordingly.

Topic Files as an Organizational Tool for the Classroom
Susie Tummers

As it is in almost any career, organization is essential to success in teaching. The organizational tool that has proved to be most beneficial during my career is my system of *topic files*. As a beginning teacher, I collected the work that I did for a particular class and placed all of it in a three-ring binder. Difficulty arose in subsequent years when I attempted to locate a particular lesson or activity. The binder was quite full, and locating specific items became a problem; hence, the topic-file strategy was born.

For each course I teach, I make a list of topics. I place these topics in file folders to start my hanging-file system. Each folder contains activities, lessons, worksheets, and so on, that pertain to that topic. When the time comes to teach a certain topic, I can easily locate the folder that contains a collection of all the information I have on that subject and begin to plan my lesson.

I have found three significant benefits to maintaining topic files. First, the files are an effective organizational tool. All topics are organized, and each file is within quick reach. If an activity or lesson focuses on more than one topic, I can easily make a few photocopies and place the duplicate information in as many topic files as is appropriate. Second, topic files provide a place for me to keep the lessons that colleagues share with me and, in turn, enable me to share ideas with colleagues. I am delighted when teachers come to my classroom asking whether I have a file on a particular topic. Third, the files are a wonderful way to organize the material I receive at the professional development conferences that I attend. When I return from a conference, I simply place photocopies of the lessons and notes in the appropriate files.

Topic files offer an organizational strategy that can work for beginning teachers at all grade levels and in all disciplines. This flexible system can easily be tailored to suit your specific needs, modified to accommodate textbook changes, or moved if you transfer to a new school. This simple idea may seem trivial, but it is one that I wish I had learned earlier in my own career.

Student Data Are As Close As Your Clipboard

Denise Mewborn
Patricia Huberty

The idea is simple: Use index cards arranged on a clipboard as a mechanism for recording information gathered during mathematics class about students' learning or management issues. You will need a clipboard, index cards (experiment with the size to find out what works for your class size and the information you want to gather), and tape. Write a student's name in bold ink at the bottom of the first index card. Tape this card at the bottom of the clipboard by placing a piece of tape at the top of the index card. Add another card by placing it on top of the first card and sliding it up so that the student's name on the bottom card is visible. Continue in this manner until you have added a card for each student. To protect the privacy of the student whose card is first, place a blank card on top (as illustrated in fig. 1). If you teach multiple classes, record the name of the class on the top index card.

A wealth of information can be recorded on each card while checking students' homework, monitoring group work, or observing students at the board. As a card becomes full, remove it and replace it with a new one. The used card can go in a file, to be used later for progress reports, report cards, student conferences, parent conferences, staffing meetings, or other times when records are needed. In instances in which students travel to another teacher, the clipboard can travel with them to serve as a communication tool between teachers.

Fig. 1.
The finished clipboard

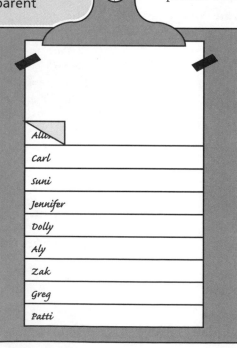

TIPS

TIPS AND ADVICE FOR BEGINNING TEACHERS

Carolyn L. Pinchback
Kathi Sweere
Sara Dean

As educators we realize that teaching involves more than what is actually taught in the classroom. We conducted a survey asking teachers for their advice or tips for new teachers. They suggested the following ideas:

1. *Always be prepared; classroom control is very important. Always remain calm.* If students think that the teacher is not prepared or not organized, they are likely to get out of control by entertaining themselves.

2. *Compliment the student's effort.* Such encouragement will result in the student's working harder to "please" the teacher.

3. *Keep the students from bothering others when they finish their work.* Having a mathematics center or a variety of mathematics workstations in which students can work when they have completed assignments may allow them to use their extra energy in a positive manner.

4. *Be consistent in dealing with students.* Students tend to remember better when the rules remain the same.

5. *Learn to write grants to obtain materials for the classroom.* Grants aid in expanding your professional development experiences and can be profitable for both you and your students.

TIPS

TIPS AND TIDBITS FOR CLASSROOM MANAGEMENT

Danielle Legnard

The following are a few tips that I wish I had learned before I became a teacher! Many of them are ongoing routines that help make my classroom a safe, risk-free environment!

Sign Language

I rarely raise my voice because I use sign language to get students' attention; have them line up, quiet down, or say "please," "thank you," or "sorry"; and even tell them what to do next! Sign language is a part of our everyday routine in my classroom!

Classical Music

The sounds of soft flutes, tiptoeing pianos, and magical strings fill the background during engaging mathematics lessons. Throughout the day, classical music fills the air as students explore, investigate, share, reason, and wonder.

Posters

Posters display important messages in my classroom; one is "The most important rule in mathematics is, You can always change your mind." This rule has become a very important part of the mathematical conversations in my classroom. Students feel safe when they know that they can always say, "I would like to change my mind!"

Thumbs Up

In my classroom students put "thumbs up" in front of their chest when they have an idea to share. This approach ensures that I can see who has an idea; the student feels acknowledged, and other students in the class have time to think through their own responses!

The Sandwich

A "sandwich" in my classroom is stating a disagreement between two positive comments! For example, a student might say, "I really like your strategy, but I don't agree with the second step and would like a chance to share mine. You always have good ideas to share." By using the sandwich idea, my students have learned to respect one another's thoughts!

Clock Buddies

When I begin a cooperative mathematics lesson, I have my students refer to their "clock-buddy clock" on their desks. Each student has a laminated copy of a clock with each hour filled in with a different student's name (e.g., John at 1:00, Tom at 2:00, Lisa at 3:00). That is, next to each hour mark, a given student has a potential "appointment" with another "clock buddy" in the class; both the student and his or her buddy must be named at the same hour on each other's clock. I simply call out a time, and students look at their clocks to see who will be their partner!

Grouping Techniques
Ideas from Adventure Education

Diana S. Perdue

I regularly use three grouping techniques in my classrooms: "pair-ups," the "song method," and the "missing-piece method." The first technique is used primarily to pair students, but groups of three or four are also possible with this method; I use the other two techniques primarily to make groups of three to five students.

Technique 1: Pair-Ups

The "pair ups" technique has many variations. Generally, I have students stand and hold up one hand, displaying from one to five fingers. Then they mingle around the room and find a partner according to a particular mathematical "rule" that I announce (e.g., the sum of their combined fingers is odd [even]). If the "rule" chosen is more challenging (e.g., the sum of their combined fingers is prime [composite]; the product of their fingers is a multiple of 4), then the students are asked to hold up both hands, displaying a number of fingers from one to ten. The "rule" can be relaxed if the last two people remaining do not meet the given condition. Students tend to concentrate on the fingers so much that they do not notice their partners until they are already together. I have also used the "pair-ups" technique with more personal conditions (e.g., the same number of siblings; the same color eyes; different kind of shoes). This grouping technique requires little advanced preparation, and one advantage is that it often leads to a review of mathematical terminology (i.e. *composite*).

Technique 2: The Song Method

The "song method" technique requires advanced preparation of certain materials. You need to prepare cards (index cards cut in halves or fourths) or slips of paper (laminated if you wish to reuse them) with names of common, well-known songs on them. Select songs to which your students will likely know the tune (not necessarily the words), for instance, "Row, Row, Row Your Boat," "Twinkle, Twinkle, Little Star," or "Frosty the Snowman." If you wish to form, for example,

five groups in all, then you will need five different songs. If you wish your groups to have, for example, four members each, then you will need four cards with the same song written on each. In class, instruct students to stand and form a circle around you. They are to draw a card from a bag and *not* show it to anyone. A good idea is to instruct your students not to "fold, spindle, or mutilate" their card while waiting for everyone to draw. Alleviate any anxiety the students might have upon reading their card by telling them that they must "know it, but not the words." Inform them that this instruction will not make sense until they read their card. After everyone has drawn a card, check that each student "knows it, but *not* the words"—do not give away anything at this point by stating something like "You have to know only the tune," because the students do not know that everyone has drawn a song title like they have. If a student responds by telling you that he or she does not know what is on their card, allow them to draw again or trade cards with a willing student. Instruct students that, on the count of three, they are to start humming as loud as possible what is on their card while mingling around the classroom seeking out those humming their same tune. When they have found someone humming the same song, they are to stop moving and continue humming until they have assembled a complete group. The "song method" is a great ice-breaker to do before a difficult project and an entertaining, nonthreatening way to group students randomly.

Technique 3: The Missing-Piece Method

The "missing piece method" is a third grouping technique that I use. It also requires advanced preparation. In a bag or some other container, place items that are cut or neatly torn into pieces distinct enough that students will be able to match them without confusion. Some items could include leaves, playing cards, old worksheets, and the like. The number of cut pieces should match the number of group members. The task is for each person to find other people having

Grouping Techniques —Continued

the missing pieces to create a complete item. A nice enhancement is to read from Shel Silverstein's (1976) book *The Missing Piece* during this activity.

These and other similar grouping techniques are often used in Adventure Education. They can also have great benefit in the classroom because they can be used to form random student groups in an objective fashion that minimizes complaints, allows students to relax about the partnerships, and even introduces some fun into the mathematics class.

Notes:

TOP TEN THINGS I WISH I HAD KNOWN
—*Cynthia Thomas*

No one can manage portfolios, projects, journals, creative writing, and student self-assessment all at the same time and stay sane! The task of assessing all these assignments is totally unreasonable to expect of yourself as a beginning teacher. If you want to incorporate these types of exercises into your teaching, pick one for this year and make it a priority in your classroom. Then, next year or even the year after that, when you are comfortable with the one extra assignment you picked, you can incorporate another innovation into your teaching.

4

EQUITY

As a beginning teacher, you will need to think about how to achieve equity in your mathematics classroom. An important resource to consult in your efforts is the Equity Principle in *Principles and Standards for School Mathematics* (NCTM 2000). This principle offers a broad outline for implementing practices that serve all students. This section complements that discussion by introducing several important ideas to consider for the students who may enter your classroom from diverse backgrounds. In particular, be aware of the issues outlined in the following paragraphs.

Evaluate Your Own Beliefs and Biases

Evaluating your own beliefs about, and biases toward, school mathematics as a discipline and about your students' learning of school mathematics is essential. To begin your reflection, you might ask yourself the following questions and try to answer candidly:

- How do I learn mathematics?

- What are some ways in which my students learn mathematics most effectively?

- Do I believe that only certain students in my classroom can learn mathematics? If so, why do I hold those beliefs?

- What expectations do I hold for my students?

- Do my beliefs and biases limit my students' opportunities to learn mathematics?

- How might I change my beliefs and biases to ensure that I promote opportunities for my students to learn mathematics?

Most likely, your responses to these types of questions will dictate your daily teaching practices and habits. As you become more aware of equity issues and more committed to making necessary accommodations to "promote access and attainment for all students" (NCTM 2000, p. 12), your own beliefs may change; in turn, you will influence your students' beliefs through the expectations you convey to them about their learning of mathematics.

Consider the Commitment

Beginning and experienced teachers alike should realize that maintaining educational equity requires a substantial commitment. You may be called on to invest considerable time and energy in activities to ensure equitable conditions in your classroom and school. Whether alone or with colleagues, you should brainstorm strategies to ensure fairness in your teaching and implementation of school policies and curricula. You may have to collaborate with colleagues to develop better understandings of the "strengths and needs of students who come from diverse linguistic and cultural backgrounds, who have specific disabilities, or who possess a special talent and interest in mathematics" (NCTM 2000, p. 14). Certainly, you should explore the literature about equity issues to continue your professional growth in this area and increase your sense of dedication to your students' mathematical achievement.

Teach Students, Then the Subject

Initially, this perspective may seem awkward, but keep in mind that regardless of the subject or the students' backgrounds, you are first teaching *individuals*. Establishing a good rapport with your students and setting high academic expectations for them are important. Further, you should vary the ways in which you conduct mathematics instruction to ensure that students relate to your teaching and perform to your levels of expectation.

Learn More about Equity Issues

Examine the readings in this section to learn more about teaching mathematics to females, students who have special needs, and culturally diverse students, including English-language learners. These readings may shed light on your understanding of the strengths and needs of students who look, speak, or behave differently than you did as a student or than you do now as an adult.

Addressing the Needs of All Students in the Elementary Mathematics Classroom

Julia A. Sliva and Mary Fay-Zenk

New teachers, along with their more experienced counterparts, face many questions when they begin to plan and assess for teaching students in today's classrooms. Among these considerations are the following: What are the main difficulties that students encounter when learning mathematics? What are some instructional strategies that I can use to facilitate understanding for various learners? And, how do I begin to plan and assess the mathematical needs of all students in my class?

Identifying the Special Learner's Needs: The Example of Sandra

Sandra usually comes into the classroom quietly and complies with requests without fussing or arguing. She turns in mathematics homework most days, but many of her solutions are incorrect or incomplete. Although class time is given to reviewing these problems, Sandra never asks a question. In fact, she avoids eye contact with you and relates comfortably with only two other girls in the class. You notice that she is often absent on test or quiz days; moreover, she makes no effort to make up these graded assessments. How can you evaluate Sandra's work and measure what Sandra understands? What is keeping her from participating in class and making improvements?

Sandra serves as an example of one of the most difficult type of students to help in the regular classroom. The less you see of Sandra's work, the less you are clearly aware of her needs and how to meet them. The resistant learner who causes few behavioral problems is often left alone. Your challenge as a teacher is to try to discover what attitudinal, perceptual, or processing issues cause some students to withdraw in the classroom setting. What approaches would help promote a positive attitude in Sandra toward learning mathematics? What intervention tactics would

increase Sandra's participation in learning and her willingness to develop strategies around problem solving?

Issues of Concern for Special Learners

The following are some of the issues that may interfere with a student's ability to learn mathematics:

- Understanding such concepts as *first, greater than*
- Remembering information
- Mentally shifting from one task to the next
- Developing essential perceptual skills, for example, spatial relationships, size relationships, and sequencing
- Developing fluency with mathematics facts
- Maintaining positive attitudes toward learning mathematics
- Selecting appropriate strategies to solve problems
- Developing facility with abstract reasoning

Support Strategies for Special Learners

Research has found several strategies to be effective for all learners, including Sandra and other reluctant learners in our classrooms. The following are some of these strategies:

- Preteaching vocabulary
- Using concrete manipulatives to teach abstract concepts
- Using multiple representations
- Using real-world applications
- Modeling problem solving
- Promoting a positive attitude toward learning mathematics
- Assisting students to develop strategies independently
- Increasing students' exposure to material

Assessing Special Learners

An important precept to remember is that any assessment of an individual student's skills must be made in relation to a wide range of mathematical content such as that recommended in the NCTM *Principles and Standards for*

School Mathematics document (2000). Once a mathematical profile is established, you need to design appropriate instructional activities that are sensitive to the learning differences of the particular student.

Understanding the Teacher's Role

Recent research has found that both curriculum design and teacher behavior directly influence the mathematics achievement of students, especially students who may have special needs. Success in solving mathematics problems is not based solely on one's knowledge of mathematics. It is also based on processes related to the use of mathematics strategies, the emotions an individual feels when doing a problem, and personal beliefs in one's mathematical abilities. Thus a thorough understanding of your students, their special needs, and their relationship to the curriculum is essential. Equally significant is instilling in your students the belief that they can and will be successful at learning important mathematics.

Research Findings Involving English-Language Learners and Implications for Mathematics Teachers

Sylvia Celedón-Pattichis

To help you build support for English-language learners in your classroom, the following paragraphs describe some terminology and research findings that address language-acquisition issues affecting mathematics teaching and learning.

Learning Language through Silence

English-language learners need a *silent period* (Baker 2001), that is, time to acquire the new language without necessarily producing it. This period often lasts two to five months and can be as long as a year. This silence should not be interpreted as unwillingness to participate in mathematics classroom activities. Teachers might use cooperative learning or pairing of students to ensure that English-language learners are exposed to the new language in nonthreatening ways.

Acquiring Social and Academic Language

English-language learners usually acquire basic interpersonal communication skills, or the *social language*, on the playground, through peer conversations, and in other informal settings during their first two years in a new culture. However, they need five to seven years or more to use the academic language required in educational content areas. The ability to use the language needed to perform in an educational context is referred to as *cognitive academic language proficiency* (Cummins, as cited in Baker [2001]).

Basic interpersonal communication skills are usually learned in *context-embedded* situations. For example, the act of talking face-to-face and using nonverbal gestures with students gives them instant feedback and clues to support spoken language. In contrast, cognitive academic language proficiency tends to be *context reduced*, meaning that no clues are available to support comprehension. Mathematics is often taught abstractly, but for English-language learners, the subject must be put into context with, for example, diagrams or the students' own definitions, especially when students are being introduced to new vocabulary and word problems.

Developing the Mathematics Register

The *mathematics register* (Halliday 1978), or the specific language used in mathematics, is often problematic for English-language learners. Contrary to popular belief, mathematics is not a universal language. The mathematics register contains many words that have different meanings from what students initially expect. Educators should distinguish between the meanings of words that overlap in the everyday use of English and in mathematics. Teachers can use many strategies to develop the mathematics register in their students, including reinterpreting words in the everyday language, such as *point, reduce, carry, set, power,* and *root*.

Making Appropriate Placements

The Third International Mathematics and Science Study indicates that the U.S. eighth-grade mathematics curriculum is at a seventh-grade level in comparison with that of other countries (United States Department of

Education 1997). Thus, care should be taken in placing English-language learners in mathematics classes to avoid repetition of content. Follow these procedures when determining placement of students from other countries:

- Use test results as supplementary information only.

- Ensure that students have a translator who can help them understand examination instructions and that the translator explains the purpose of the test results.

- If a textbook is available, compare and contrast the curriculum used in the student's previous country with that used in your state or district.

- Negotiate possible placements by talking to teachers, parents, the student, and counselors. If the student needs to take a mathematics course that is offered at a higher grade level, then the school district should make that option available.

- Ask for previous school contact information from the student or the family to learn what mathematical skills the student demonstrated in his or her previous school.

Sharing Learners' Cultures in the Classroom

To establish a positive learning environment, mathematics educators should consider the linguistic and cultural experiences that English-language learners bring to the classroom. For example, if a student uses a different algorithm for division, demonstrate it to the class to create a learning moment for everyone. Finally, research students' backgrounds and seek the help of bilingual teachers or specialists in English as a second language to help your students adjust to their new culture.

Mathematics Instruction That Works for Girls

Abbe H. Herzig
Rebecca Ambrose
Olof Steinthorsdottir

Mathematics instruction has traditionally catered to a small segment of the population. We encourage you to consider some of the following suggestions gleaned from educational research for making your mathematics instruction accessible to all students, especially girls.

Vary instructional strategies

Discourse has become an important element in mathematics classes, but it does not always have to be conducted in a whole-class setting. Students who are less assertive or less confident about speaking publicly—as many girls are—are less likely to participate actively in whole-class discussions. Working cooperatively with their peers in small groups gives students opportunities to engage actively in mathematics in a less threatening environment.

Too often, mathematics classes become the site of competition, with students being encouraged to be the fastest and the brightest. Some students, including many females, find this kind of competition distasteful and resist participating in it. Group work can create a supportive environment in which the emphasis is on learning together instead of surpassing other students. Many girls prefer this environment.

Although individual seatwork or whole-class discussions might work best for certain types of lessons, group work is often an effective way to engage all students in performing high-quality mathematics tasks. Different students flourish in different environments, and by varying the types of work you do in class, you give more students opportunities to do their best.

TOP TEN THINGS I WISH I HAD KNOWN
—*Cynthia Thomas*

Some days you will cry, but the good news is, some days you will laugh! Learn to laugh with your students and at yourself!

3

Focus on understanding and problem solving

When mathematics is taught as an abstract set of rules and recipes for solving various categories of problems, students learn to solve those specific problems but may not be able to use that knowledge in other contexts. Some research suggests that even though all students, boys and girls, prefer to understand the mathematics they are studying, girls will distance themselves from mathematics when they do not understand it, whereas boys are less bothered by a lack of understanding. When students learn mathematics with understanding, they are able to use that knowledge as a foundation for further learning.

Instead of focusing on correct answers, make problem-solving strategies the primary emphasis of your instruction. By examining your students' strategies, you will start to learn what they understand and can plan future instruction accordingly. Encourage your students to explain their reasoning and to actively listen to, question, and learn from, one another. They will discover that mathematics makes sense, and more students will maintain their interest in the subject.

Make mathematics meaningful

Students who do not see the use for mathematics are less likely to stay interested in it. Girls seem to be particularly sensitive to issues of relevance in mathematics. Problems that are set in meaningful contexts can be excellent motivation for students who need to see the relevance of what they do. The contexts chosen should be interesting and relevant to all students in your class, both girls and boys. Too often, mathematics problems focus on topics that interest boys, without a balance of problems that appeal to girls. As you get to know your students, you can choose problem contexts that are most meaningful to them; doing so can also be a great way to engage students of diverse ethnic backgrounds. You can also ask students to write problems for others in the class to solve. This exercise can be a helpful way to involve students, learn how they think about mathematics, and develop meaningful problem contexts.

Use a deliberate strategy for calling on students

In whole-class discussions, boys tend to raise their hands faster than girls. If you call on the first person who responds to a question, you leave out those students who require more time to think about the question and formulate responses. Research shows that girls still tend to be less assertive and may need time to develop confidence before raising their hands. Experiment with different strategies for getting more students involved in class discussions. Always give students plenty of time to think before calling on anyone. You might try silently counting to ten before choosing a student to respond to a question. You might also call out names for responses instead of choosing students who have raised their hands, to ensure that everyone has equal opportunities to participate.

Examine the types of feedback you give students

Some research shows that teachers interact with students in different ways—most likely, without realizing it. In responding to students' work, teachers sometimes ask boys more sophisticated and challenging questions than they ask girls. Because most teachers are probably unaware of this behavior, we should all continually reflect on how we talk to our students. Be sure to reward all students' progress equally and ask them all questions that challenge them to think more deeply about mathematics.

Maintain high expectations for all students

Research shows that when teachers have different expectations for different students, their interactions with students reflect those expectations. If a teacher does not believe that a student has high potential—because of the student's race, gender, disability, or ethnicity, for example—then the teacher may be satisfied with a lower level of performance from that individual than from a student who the teacher thinks is more capable. Further, students are likely to live up, or down, to the teacher's expectations. In your classroom, maintain high expectations for all students because all are capable of learning mathematics with understanding.

Tips for Teaching Culturally Diverse Students

Joan Cohen Jones

As a beginning mathematics teacher, I taught in a culturally and ethnically diverse district in the southeastern United States. My students were recent immigrants from

Africa, Asia, and Mexico. Our soccer team had representatives from seventeen countries, and our PTA newsletter was printed in nine languages. During my first year, I remember becoming frustrated with a Cambodian student who would not look at me when I spoke to him. Only later did I learn that in his culture, this behavior was a sign of respect rather than disrespect. This experience helped me realize that my lack of knowledge about students' cultural backgrounds hampered my ability to communicate with them effectively.

While I learned more about my students' cultures, I also developed effective strategies for teaching mathematics to diverse students. The following tips are drawn from my experiences as a teacher, student-teaching supervisor, and teacher educator. These strategies can work for all students, but they are specifically designed to create positive experiences for culturally diverse students. They are appropriate for all grade levels and can easily be adapted to other disciplines.

Check for existing knowledge

When planning for instruction, decide what concepts students need to know to learn the new material. Include checks for existing knowledge at the beginning of your lessons. If necessary, restructure your lessons to develop the requisite knowledge.

Listen to what students say

Listen to students' comments, questions, and responses. Only by listening carefully can you learn what your students know, what they misunderstand, what is important for them to learn, and what are the best ways for them to learn.

Question students to reinforce learning and build students' confidence

Ask questions to reinforce students' learning, for example, "How do you know?" "Who knows how to find the answer?" "Will that approach always work?" "Have you seen other problems like this one before?" "Can you find a pattern?" Such questions encourage students to give explanations, search for connections, and rely on themselves and their peers, building self-reliance, cooperation, respect, and confidence.

Increase wait time during classroom discourse

Increasing your wait time during classroom discourse enhances your listening and questioning skills and improves communication. When listening to students' questions, for example, wait until they are finished speak-

ing instead of cutting in after you think you know what is being asked. Pause for several seconds before trying to answer the question yourself or asking someone else to answer it. Then repeat the question to make sure that you understand what is being asked. When a teacher really listens, students are encouraged to ask the questions they might otherwise keep to themselves. Being given extra time to answer can also be helpful to female students and students whose first language is not English.

Respect students' abilities and competence

Demonstrate respect for your students' abilities and competence by giving them high-level intellectual tasks that require complex processing and critical thinking. Doing so conveys your confidence that they can master the material.

Become familiar with and respect students' cultures

Find out as much as possible about each culture represented in your class. Parents and other family members are wonderful resources to help you learn about your students' backgrounds. If possible, spend some time in the neighborhood in which your school is located. Shop at the local grocery store, participate in neighborhood festivals and celebrations, eat at local restaurants, and become familiar with community activities. This practice can enhance your cultural understanding.

Be reflective

Become a reflective practitioner. That is, monitor, review, and revise your practices, instructional choices, and methodology consistently to ensure that you are being fair and open-minded, providing high-level tasks for your students, and connecting your students' cultural backgrounds with new concepts. An important step in reflection is to think about your own cultural heritage and understand your own biases. Reflection lets you review your own actions in light of what you know about yourself, including your strengths, weaknesses, biases, and prejudices. Some teachers find that keeping a journal, making records of class discussions, or videotaping their classroom instruction is helpful in this process.

Offer students choices

Offer your students instructional choices. Student choice is especially important for culturally diverse students, who may have learning styles that differ from those of their peers in the dominant culture. When developing classroom activities, offer choices in assignments and types of assessments; give students the opportunity to work independently, in pairs, or in small groups; and allow students to respond in oral or written form, individually, in teams, or as a class.

Enjoy the challenge

Teaching mathematics to diverse students can be challenging but extremely rewarding—both personally and professionally. I hope the ideas discussed here are helpful as you begin your career in education.

Bringing High Expectations to Life in an Urban Classroom

Ido Jamar
Vanessa R. Pitts

We often hear that one of the most challenging issues facing beginning teachers is classroom management. Although this statement is true for teachers in any setting, it is especially true for beginning teachers in urban classrooms. Clearly learning cannot take place in a classroom that is out of control, but are rules and regulations all that are needed to foster an optimal learning setting for urban students? Haberman (1991) found that "urban schools that serve as models of student learning have teachers who maintain control by establishing trust and involving their students in meaningful activities [therefore] … discipline and control are primarily a *consequence* of their teaching and not a *prerequisite* condition of learning" (p. 293).

Maintaining High Expectations for All

Unfortunately, whether a teacher engages students in meaningful, challenging tasks often depends on how the teacher perceives the abilities of the students. Too often, minority students have been victims of teachers' low expectations, with the result that students' achievement has mirrored those expectations. High expectations manifested through both words and deeds are necessary if *all* students are to reach high levels of mathematics achievement.

Conveying Expectations to Students

Many facets of teaching can send students a subtle message that tells them that you hold high expectations for them. For example,

a) by providing opportunities for students to understand concepts prior to learning rules, you make it clear that you know they *can* understand the content and that it is understandable;

b) by using students' existing knowledge as building blocks for new knowledge, you let them know that they already have the necessary foundation needed to learn; and

c) by expecting students to be active participants in their own learning, you make it clear that they are to take responsibility for their own learning.

Although these pedagogical practices are consistent with current reform recommendations, they also create a space in which academic excellence can become the norm, not the exception, for minority students (Ladson-Billings 1994).

Notes:

6 SECTION

SCHOOL AND COMMUNITY

Although you will undoubtedly find yourself very busy in your first year of teaching, you will need to find time to reach out to parents and the surrounding school community. In addition to learning more about your students, you will discover that establishing relationships with parents and the community will yield the resources and support required to be successful. When teachers, parents, and the community act together, students benefit in numerous ways. This cooperation often leads to increased rates of attendance, improved academic achievement and graduation rates, and generally better attitudes about school.

Parents are your students' first teachers and your greatest resource. Parents can provide you with valuable information about their children's interests, attitudes, environment, habits, and aptitudes. Parents can be your staunch allies and partners, encouraging their children to persevere and achieve in mathematics. To tap this important resource, often, you only have to reach out and invite parents into a partnership. The same approach also works for members of the community and other significant adults in your students' lives. Encouraging and valuing their contributions strengthen and reinforce their involvement.

As you plan for the school year, develop a strategy to encourage and nurture these vital partnerships. You can start on a small scale by—

- holding regular parent meetings and conferences;
- recruiting classroom volunteers to serve as tutors, guest speakers, and general classroom helpers;
- establishing a school-home connection with homework;
- publishing a parent newsletter; and
- welcoming parents, grandparents, or other involved adults to school.

In this section, you will find other suggestions about how to begin this process, including tips on communicating with parents, sharing your ideas with them, and involving them in the mathematics education of their children. Begin formulating your plan by reviewing these suggestions and reflecting on how they might work for you. Develop goals for parental and community involvement, and jot down notes about how you might accomplish these goals. Talk with your mentor and colleagues about their strategies, and seek out additional resources, such as *Involving Families in School Mathematics: Readings from "Teaching Children Mathematics," "Mathematics Teaching in the Middle School," and "Arithmetic Teacher,"* available from NCTM (Edge 2000). Most of all, develop a positive relationship with the families of your students. Doing so is a rewarding experience and well worth the investment of your time.

Suggestions to Welcome Parents into the Mathematics Classroom

Denise Edelson

Get your students' parents involved in your mathematics instruction. Do not assume that they are aware of the latest research, methods, or standards in teaching. Most parents have only their personal elementary mathematics experiences as a reference point; chances are these experiences did not include manipulatives, authentic instruction, or an integrated curriculum. Parents should have some point of connection with the program that you are implementing with their children. Accordingly, invite parents into your classroom for a time of mathematics learning, and give them a taste of the components of your thoughtful, standards-based program. The following are some suggestions.

Suggestions to welcome parents into the classroom

- Parents will come to your classroom if they feel comfortable. Reassure them. I suggest that you invite parents into your classroom during a school day and let them sit with their child. Some parents may feel very inadequate and worry that they will be unable to complete even a primary-grade mathematics assignment on their own. Reassure them that they will not be judged on their work. Feed them. Food is comforting and friendly. I send out party invitations and present an "M&M's mathematics" lesson at my first parent gathering. Everyone happily eats candy at the end of the lesson. I make sure to serve good treats at all my mathematics events.

- Parents will do almost anything because they love their child. In thinking of activities that are interesting and entertaining to parents, I get concerned that parents might become bored from, or disdainful of, doing primary-grade work with their child. But I have discovered that parents are just happy to be attending the event with their child, because by doing so, they show their child that they care. Now, although I still present activities that I think the parents might enjoy, I have stopped worrying about entertaining them.

- Parents want you to love their child, too. Parents sometimes hear only unflattering things about their child at school—what he or she needs to do to improve or to behave appropriately. They may wonder whether the teacher even likes their child. An informal mathematics gathering is an opportunity to talk about a child's strengths and abilities. Compliment individual students on their patterning-block pictures, unit-cube patterns, and bean sorting. Their parents will beam and be more likely to calmly accept suggestions for improvement at another meeting, because you have shown that you care and have demonstrated that you can see strengths in their child.

- Parents want to be more involved, but they do not always get good information from their children about what is happening at school. A face-to-face meeting is your chance to show parents that hands-on mathematics is not just "play" despite what their children have told them after school. Your students' parents will be more supportive of your program when they have had opportunities to understand how play translates into mathematical experiences.

- Parents want their children to succeed, in spite of what parents may do or say. They will take afternoons off from work (Friday afternoons worked for me.) to attend an important school activity.

- Parents learn in similar ways as children learn. Do not just tell parents about the wonderful materials that you are using in your classroom. Get out those counters or any other manipulatives, and give the parents a hands-on lesson; read them an entertaining children's mathematics trade book, show a portion of a good mathematics video, set up interest centers that children can explain to their parents, and post information about pieces-per-serving and calorie count near the cookies (mathematical connections that can be carried into the home). While the children eat cookies, visit with the parents and joyfully talk about…mathematics!

Calling Home:
Keeping in Contact with Students' Families

Laura Brader-Araje

As a new mathematics teacher, I knew that taking on too much and trying to be perfect at everything would leave me only heartache and stress. For this reason, I decided to be selective in my goal setting for the beginning year. Included in my plan was my hope to develop a system to track communications with the parents and guardians of my students. I knew that the primary method of communication between teachers and students' families at that time was the telephone. Thus, keeping track of incoming and outgoing calls to students' homes would be the basis of any system I would devise.

The System

I decided on an index card system, which may sound simple or even archaic, but what a gem this scheme was for me! I taught five classes, and in my system, each class was coded with a different colored card. For example, period 1 was yellow, period 2 was blue, and so on. Each student was initially allocated a single note card, listing his or her name, parents' or guardians' names, and home and work telephone numbers. I alphabetized the cards in a large index card file.

My Proactive Approach

To initiate positive relationships with all these parents, I took a proactive approach; I decided to go to the parents before they came to me. To do so, I tried to make at least five phone calls a day, leaving messages on machines more often than actually hearing another person on the other end of the line: "Hello, my name is Laura Brader, and I am your daughter's new mathematics teacher. I am calling to introduce myself and to touch base. If you ever need anything, please give me a call at school. I look forward to meeting with you!" I could keep my home number unlisted because I was readily available before, during, and after school hours most of the time.

The Benefits

I maintained my calling routine in between returning calls from parents who had specific concerns throughout the year, because the benefits of the system clearly justified the amount of time involved. The index-card system proved useful over the course of the school year for a variety of reasons, including the following:

- I used the index cards to document the date and time of a call, the person with whom I spoke if someone was available, and the purpose of the call. This record gave me evidence to address problems and to use in team meetings with parents.

- The phone calls helped head off many potential problems because they gave me the chance to mention homework attempts, classroom behavior that was becoming disruptive, concerns about absences, and other issues.

- The system prompted me to call all parents over time, more than once, whether or not I had a specific reason to do so. The calls showed that I cared, and I did, about all my students, not just the infamous ones whoes parents receive phone calls each year from all their child's teachers.

- When problems arose and team meetings were called, the documentation on the index cards allowed me to clarify my approaches toward resolution.

- I created the "luxury," as one team member called it, to transform the dreaded phone call home into an opportunity to tell parents that their children had done well on a project or showed great improvement in a particular area. I found that the parents of students who do not cause problems rarely receive timely, positive feedback about their children; my phone calls provided this praise.

- The initial round of phone calls and messages gave me insight into which students erased messages from teachers before their parents came home and which students did not. I came to understand these students' experiences when teachers had "called home" in the past.

Addressing Administrators' Concerns

In my experience, new teachers often find that their actions—and inaction—are under constant scrutiny. Administrators may ask, "Have parent phone calls been returned?" "Are guardians being notified of excessive absences?" "Do students know why calls are being made to their homes?" The index cards, kept in a box by the telephone, allow new teachers to answer this barrage of questions they will receive in their first nine months on the job.

Closing Thoughts

Calling home keeps me in contact with the parents or guardians of my students and seems to help head off trouble before it starts. Documenting these interactions provides the backup or proof that teachers need in this age of accountability. Finally, a new teacher's attempts to reach out to parents when school starts and to keep in contact with them throughout the year creates a positive impression of the school and bridges the traditional gap between teacher and community.

Sharing Your Principles and Standards with Parents
Mark W. Ellis
Robert Q. Berry III

We have found that most parents, when well informed about a teacher's motives and methods, are supportive of efforts to promote higher-order thinking, conceptual understanding, mathematical communication, and authentic problem solving in the classroom. Many parents see these efforts as a refreshing change from the focus on algorithms they experienced in learning mathematics, which they may remember as a series of unrelated procedures that mysteriously transformed numbers into answers.

To generate parental support, you need to communicate the mathematical goals that you have set for students and the ways in which you are helping students achieve these goals—in essence, your own principles and standards. To help parents become knowledgeable about these goals, you may wish to send home a parent newsletter or make a presentation at a PTA meeting or school open house. You might also create an opportunity for parents to share in the mathematical experiences that their children are receiving in your classroom by hosting a family mathematics night.

These outreach efforts are important because parents who have experienced mathematics through traditional procedure-oriented instruction often have questions about teaching strategies that you may apply in your classroom, for example, cooperative work, student inquiry, manipulative modeling, and writing assignments. Also, consider sharing with parents research findings that support NCTM Standards–based instruction. Parents will see firsthand how Standards-based practices enhance students' understanding and enable them to attach meaning to mathematical concepts and ideas.

TOP TEN THINGS I WISH I HAD KNOWN
—*Cynthia Thomas*

2

You will make mistakes. You cannot undo your mistakes, but berating yourself for them is counterproductive. If the mistake requires an apology, make it and move on. No one is keeping score.

Bulletin Board Idea: Student History Time Lines

Debra Daniels

Consider making your bulletin boards personal for students, containing items that are not dated so that the items can stay posted for a length of time.

One great idea is to have students make personal history time lines. Doing so is an excellent way to get to know all your students at the beginning of the year. Some students may include personal photographs, others may write points of interest, and some may draw pictures of their personal milestones. I usually request that the time lines be completed as a family home project. As students bring in their finished projects, I give them time to share their histories with the class so that they can get to know one another on a more personal level. We cover the walls and halls with these time lines. They make great displays for our fall open house and are enjoyed by many people for a long time.

Things I Never Learned in Methods Class: Support Staff

Do not take the school secretaries or custodians for granted. Remember their names, and greet them with smiles. Also, remember to express appreciation for the work they do.

—*Margaret R. Meyer*

Notes:

TOP TEN THINGS I WISH I HAD KNOWN
—*Cynthia Thomas*

1

This *is* the best job on earth! Stand up straight! Hold your head high! Look people in the eye and proudly announce, "I am a teacher!"

ONLINE RESOURCES FOR THE BEGINNING TEACHER

The Internet is one of the best resources available to you as a beginning teacher. As you probably already know, numerous Web sites are available for practically any instructional topic in which you are interested. A few sites serve as central clearinghouses, providing links to related sources of information. The Web sites listed below have been active for a while; they are fairly stable in terms of accessibility and are kept up-to-date with the latest educational developments. As part of your professional growth plan, explore these sites to search for information on particular topics or issues pertaining to mathematics teaching and learning. Make an attempt to visit at least one every month, if for no other reason than to learn what is happening in the educational world outside your classroom.

- For professional growth opportunities, visit the National Council of Teachers of Mathematics (NCTM) site at www.nctm.org. NCTM membership is required to gain access to some of the features.

- For instructional ideas, visit the Math Forum Web site at mathforum.org/. In particular, you might want to explore "Teacher2Teacher" for answers to your questions about teaching mathematics. You can browse the archives, search the frequently asked questions, or submit a question of your own.

- For professional publications related to the implementation of curriculum and instruction, visit the Association for Supervision and Curriculum Development site at www.ascd.org.

- For assessment information, view the searchable online journal *Practical Assessment, Research and Evaluation* at www.ericae.net/pare.

- For current research publications, browse the education category of the National Academies Press Web site at www.nap.edu.

- For a variety of publications related to education, visit the Eisenhower National Clearinghouse site at www.enc.org.

- For research and resources on general topics pertaining to various aspects of education, visit the U.S. Department of Education on the Web at www.ed.gov.

Notes:

REFERENCES

Baker, Colin. *Foundations of Bilingual Education and Bilingualism.* Philadelphia, Pa.: Multilingual Matters, 2001.

Edge, Douglas, ed. *Involving Families in School Mathematics: Readings from "Teaching Children Mathematics," "Mathematics Teaching in the Middle School," and "Arithmetic Teacher."* Reston, Va.: National Council of Teachers of Mathematics, 2000.

Feiman-Nemser, Sharon. "What New Teachers Need to Learn." *Educational Leadership* 60 (May 2003): 25–29.

Flores, Alfinio. "Electronic Technology and NCTM Standards." 1998. http://mathforum.org/technology/papers/papers/flores.html (accessed 12 April 2001).

Haberman, Martin. "The Pedagogy of Poverty versus Good Teaching." *Phi Delta Kappan* 73, no. 4 (December 1991): 290–94.

Halliday, Michael Alexander Kirkwood. *Language as Social Semiotic.* Baltimore, Md.: Edward Arnold, 1978.

Ladson-Billings, Gloria. *The Dreamkeepers: Successful Teachers of African American Children.* San Francisco: Jossey-Bass Publishers, 1994.

National Council of Teachers of Mathematics (NCTM). *Curriculum and Evaluation Standrfds for School Mathematics.* Reston, Va.: NCTM, 1989.

———. *Principles and Standards for School Mathematics.* Reston, Va.: NCTM, 2000.

Renard, Lisa. "Setting New Teachers Up for Failure…or Success." *Educational Leadership* 60 (May 2003): 62–64.

Silverstein, Shel. The Missing Piece. New York: Harper & Row, 1976.

United States Department of Education. *Introduction to TIMSS: The Third International Mathematics and Science Study.* Washington, D.C.: United States Department of Education, 1997.

Two additional titles appear in the
Empowering the Beginning Teacher of Mathematics
series
(Michaele F. Chappell, series editor):

Empowering the Beginning Teacher of Mathematics in Middle School
Edited by Michaele F. Chappell and Tina Pateracki

Empowering the Beginning Teacher of Mathematics in High School
Edited by Michaele F. Chappell, Jeffrey Choppin, and Jenny Salls

Please consult
www.nctm.org/catalog
for the availability of these titles,
as well as for a plethora of
resources for teachers of mathematics
at all grade levels.

For the most up-to-date listing of NCTM resources on topics of interest to mathematics educators, as well as information on member benefits, conferences, and workshops, visit the NCTM Web site at www.nctm.org.